DONALD E

Keys to Unlocl
for Life-Changing Results

PRESS

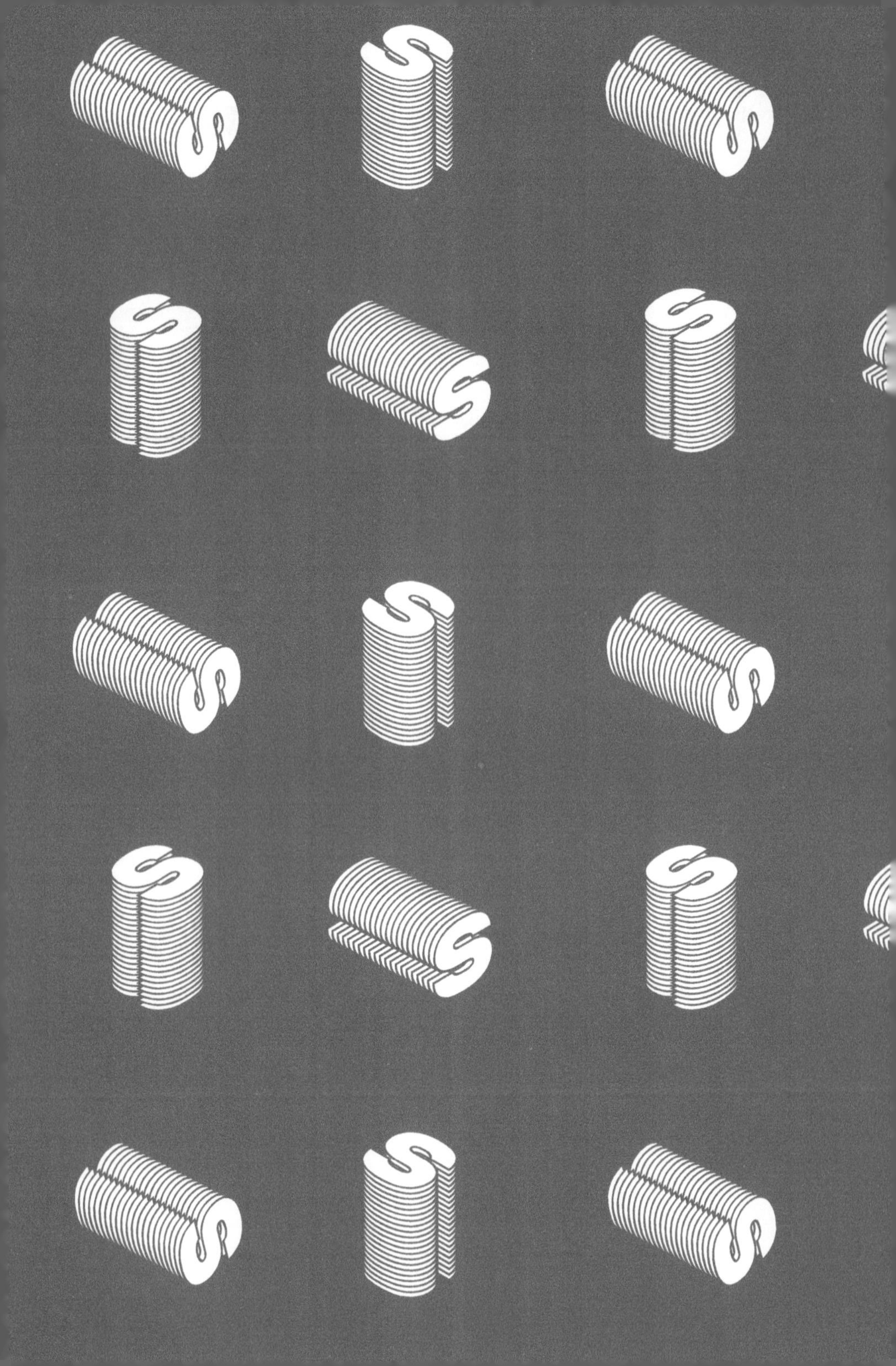

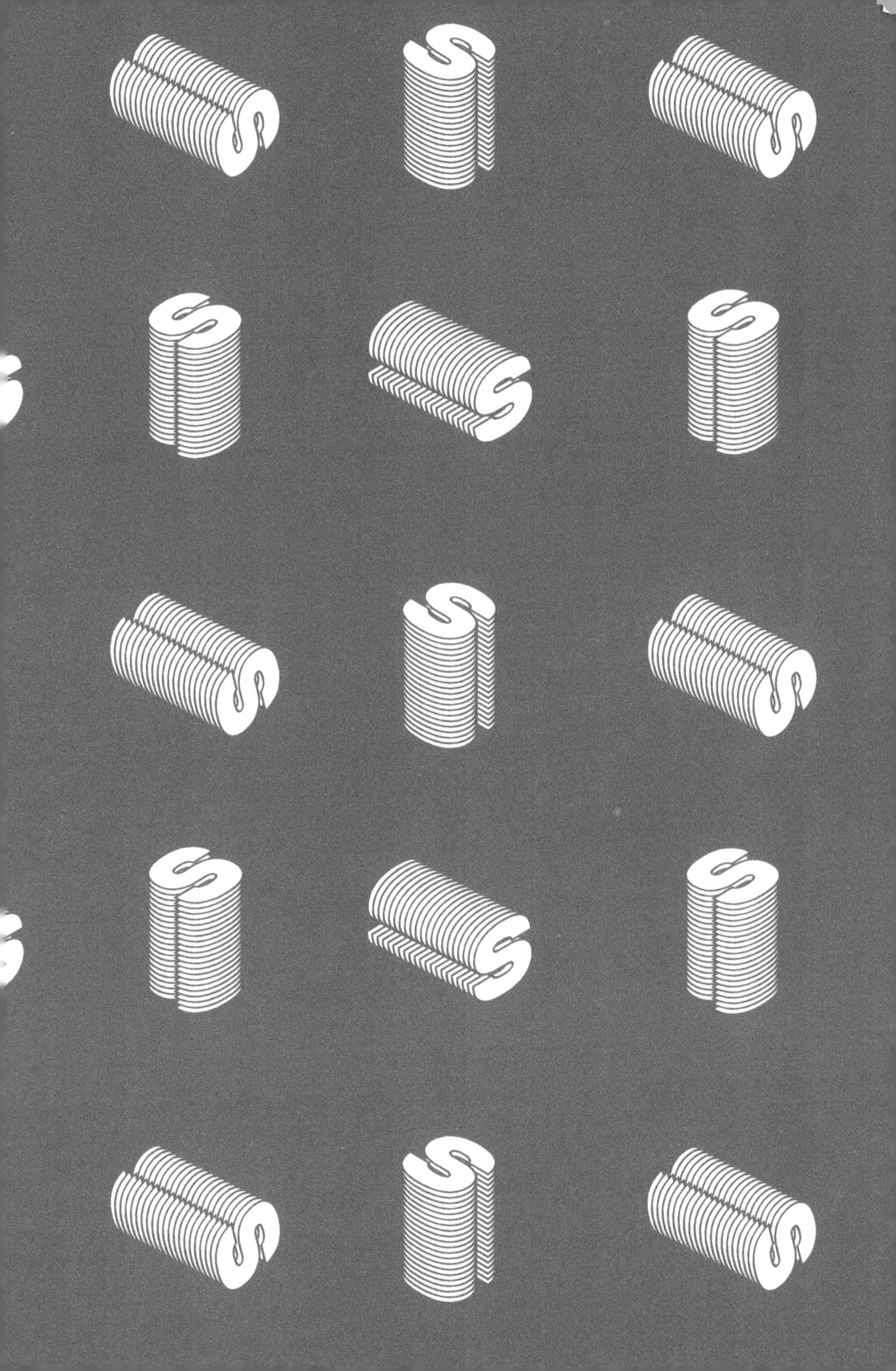

© 2020 by Donald Burlock, Jr.
All rights reserved. No part of this publication may be reproduced, distributed, or transmitted in any form or by any means, including photocopying, recording, or other electronic or mechanical methods, without the prior written permission of the publisher, except in the case of brief quotations embodied in critical reviews and certain other noncommercial uses permitted by copyright law.

Gold Coast Press, Inc.
www.superhumanbydesign.com

Book design by Venga Brands

ISBN 978-1-7357702-0-8

Printed by IngramSpark in the United States of America

To everyone in the world who has failed at something.

To everyone who has made a mistake and learned from it.

To everyone who has hurt the people they love the most.

And to everyone who has wondered about their path in life.

This book is dedicated to you—the person wanting to become more than you are today—because we all can choose to be greater.

BRIEF CONTENTS

DETAILED CONTENTS

PART ONE. CREATIVITY AND THE SUPERHUMAN LIFE

PART TWO. POWERS, PILLARS, AND RESULTS

PART THREE. GETTING STARTED: TAKEOFF

If you make yourself more than just a man, if you devote yourself to an ideal, and if they can't stop you, then you become something else entirely.

— *Batman Begins*, 2005

While many superheroes come by their superpowers through genetic blessing or freakish accident, Batman is a regular guy who gained his superhuman abilities on his own. He studied science, perfected his body, sharpened his mind and powers of deduction, and utilized technology. He became superhuman through his own effort, adding to his powers element by element.

— Brett and Kate McKay, *The Art of Manliness*

FOREWORD

The first time I met Donald, he gave me his resignation.

It was my initial week as Executive Creative Director of frog's San Francisco headquarters and, needless to say, with his resignation as a senior design leader, it was not off to an auspicious start.

I walked into the conversation thinking that my job was to win him back—to understand what was lacking for him in his role and to see what could be offered that would make him decide to stay.

That's not how it went.

Instead of a negotiation, I found myself in that rarest of all exchanges: a bone-deep, soul-to-soul meeting with a man who was absolutely present in his journey, and who was awake to and curious about my own.

That, my friend, is some superhuman-level s***.

Donald and I are designers. Simply put, we imagine a world that doesn't yet exist and, through our work, bring it into being. From the outside, design might look like *omnificence* (the superpower that gives one the ability to create anything without limit) or maybe (and less grandiosely) *earth bending*. What design really is, however, is this: a practice of intention, iteration, taste, and no small amount of optimism, a practice that is as potent in the public sphere as it is in the personal one.

The book you are holding in your hands (or reading on your screen) is for those of us who are imagining a self, or a life, that doesn't yet exist and who thrill to its potential. What Donald offers here, shared in the universal language of superheroes, is a collection of humble, iterative actions that can move those imaginings closer to reality.

You may be thinking, "But I'm no superhuman..." You're right. You're not. But as Superman would say, you're much stronger than you think you are. Trust me.

Oonie Chase

Oonie Chase, Executive Director, IDEO

PREFACE

Creativity can be undervalued.

"What?" you say. "Surely not! Just look at all the books out there on creativity. If anything, it's being oversold."

In one sense, yes. In another, most decidedly not.

Much, if not all, of what you'll see about creativity has to do with talent, with career, with individual satisfaction. This book is about all that and more.

I want you to unlock your creativity in much deeper ways, so that you can be your boldest and most successful self—in all aspects of your life. I want you to discover a new perspective on the value of creativity and to develop deep new wells of creativity from which to draw to fuel a better life, both for yourself and for those in your life who are important to you. It is this creativity, once you tap into it, that can help you become what I call *superhuman*.

I have spent the last decade as a designer at several major corporations—global brands like Coca-Cola, Dolby Laboratories, and IDEO—and even within the walls of such highly esteemed and clearly well-functioning companies, I have seen people fall short. Sometimes of the goals set for them at work. Sometimes of the needs of the people in their lives. Sometimes of their own needs and goals. To be clear, I have also fallen short of my own goals and have sometimes missed answering the needs of those important to me in my life. I am on the same path as everyone else. These failures hit home to all of us.

As a designer, it's my business to uncover problems and then to design solutions. And so I have watched and I have analyzed. And what I began to see is that, most of the time, the problem with the various sorts of personal and professional failures I was seeing could be traced to a single root: the inability of a person to unlock and harness their own creativity. I would see colleagues, for example, blocking their own path at work by downplaying a process such as brainstorming or collaborative exercises that encourage creativity. Outside of my professional life, I often hear people say, "Oh, I'm not that creative" or "Creativity is for artists."

On the flip side, I realized that the most inspiring people I met were the ones who tapped into, and operationalized, their inner creative selves. These individuals were conscious of the world around them, and they tried out different ways of generating new solutions and exciting outcomes. This strategy made them successful in all the avenues of their lives, not just in the marketplace, but in their personal lives as well. At the office, they were often the most inspirational people to work alongside, and away from work, they were often lauded for being a positive influence in their families and communities.

Seeing this, I began developing a system to explore how and why creativity is the gateway to excellence and to happiness not only in a career, but in a life. This book is the culmination of that work. *Superhuman-by-Design* comes from years of observing what works and what doesn't in real life—and from deeply exploring how anyone might apply these lessons in their own life.

I've been working to apply the concept and the system in my life. And now I'd like to help you apply it in yours.

WHO YOU ARE AND WHAT YOU WANT OUT OF LIFE

If you've picked up this book based on its title, you likely fall into one of these categories:

- → *Success-oriented:* You're seeking business and marketing growth strategies to attain new heights in your career or the marketplace.
- → *Impact-oriented:* You believe that achievements are important, but not as important as living a life of significance, one that extends beyond individual desires.
- → *Creativity-oriented:* You want to live an inspired life full of curiosity about how your talents and passions can reach and influence hundreds of people.

Or you might find that, like me, you're all three. Either serially, depending on situation and circumstance, or all at once. Every day, I find myself operating with the hunger of an entrepreneur, adding value to others and their imperatives, designing solutions that can impact many people, and searching for inspiration in the world.

If any of this sounds like you, then we are on this journey together. And exploring the concept of becoming superhuman-by-design will change your life.

MY APPROACH

I've learned a lot from my own experiences and observations, most particularly because of my design training, but I've also learned from the expertise of (as should we all!). I will draw upon both, grounding the principles in this book both in my work as a designer and on the expertise of recognized authorities, people who have spent years researching the ways the mind, body, and spirit work.

I'll illustrate those principles with some examples of real-life superhumans, as I'm using the term—people who've shown that the outcomes they've achieved are purposely built and fueled by endless wells of creativity. I want to show you that anyone can consistently deliver superhuman results, that anyone can generate significant improvements and innovative ideas for the world around them. Just for fun, I'll also weave in fictional superheroes, but only as points of departure. These characters serve to comment on the human condition, and they also reflect whom we might aspire to be and what we uphold as noble and good. Since I am a visual person, I find that using superheroes provides both a mental model and a lighthearted framework to spark our discussion of superpowers.

And this will be our discussion, our journey. Because here's the big difference between the concept of superhuman-by-design and the concepts (or strategies) in many other self-growth books: this system of principles is not a ready-made solution to be cut and pasted into your life. You must pour yourself into it and work with it to galvanize the process and make it happen. I'll give you the template, but you'll have to make it yours. That way, it will be truly yours and yours for life.

HOW THIS BOOK IS ORGANIZED

And now for a quick preview of what's to come in the book you hold in your hands.

Part One. Creativity and the Superhuman Life

In this first part, you'll explore what it means to be (in the sense I'm using it) "superhuman" and what it means to do something "by design." You'll discover why creativity is foundational to living a superhuman life, what the special relationship is between creativity and design, and how the two dovetail, each enhancing the other.

You'll delve into how to practice deeper creativity and why it's beneficial to push every day to be your best creative self. You'll study the character traits of creativity—those theoretical principles and values that act as the boundaries of the ups and downs in your journey to deeper and sustained creativity in your life. You'll have an opportunity to think about these precepts, connect with them according to your own internal sense of what's right for you, and decide how best to weave them into your life, into your journey.

Part Two. Powers, Pillars, and Results

Welcome to the heart of the book! Here's where you'll explore how to apply the superhuman-by-design concept to all areas of your life, by learning to leverage the abilities and talents you already have in you as superpowers *and* by developing new superpowers that you can phase into your life. You'll also explore the pillars you'll need to incorporate these superpowers into your everyday routines, so that you can live to your full potential.

Throughout this part, you'll explore how to channel your creative self to focus on holistic approaches to mental wellness, fitness, finance, and relationships. The goal will be to integrate everything introduced up to this point in the book, to enable you to see how to become an effective, value-adding contributor to the world around you, personally and professionally. Regardless of your personality type or preferred style to approaching external circumstances, the principles in this section are valuable, timeless, and worth adapting to what works for you.

This second part of the book is all about application. Think of it as an interactive volume that you can come back to over and over as you personalize the material. Dive right in! Grab your electronic highlighting tool and mark the passages that speak particularly to you.

Part Three. Getting Started: Takeoff

Now you're ready to begin implementing your superhuman journey. . . To lead a life in which you can overcome the paralyzing feelings created by external circumstances. To live up to your full potential every day. To push through the challenge of starting this journey and staying with it until you see progress.

You'll trace the steps you'll need to take to scale mountains in private moments and to identify the strategies you can use to applying this philosophy to your life—which means intentionally developing a practice to stabilize you no matter what obstacles you face.

This is the feet-on-the-ground, face-looking-toward-the-heavens part of the process. And now you launch.

PROLOGUE

There was a moment in 2018 when this book almost didn't happen.

I found myself in an emotional lull, questioning whether what I was writing could truly become my personal practice on a daily basis. I even wondered whether anything I might share would be worthwhile to you, the reader.

This lull seemed to find a way to keep me from picking up my pen. From opening my MacBook. From jotting thoughts down on a napkin during a long flight.

And then, just as the fog can dissipate and the skies open to gorgeous, cerulean blue in the San Francisco Bay, my lull was sent scattering by a story.

It's easy to forget how incredibly impactful a simple story can be. Especially if the person telling the story is as compelling as the story itself. When we experience such a story, its impact is unquestionable. In fact, one of my favorite books, *Made to Stick*, from authors Chip and Dan Heath, has this to say about the power of story:

> ***The story's power. . . then, is twofold: It provides simulation (knowledge about how to act) and inspiration (motivation to act). Note that both benefits, simulation and inspiration, are geared to generating* action.**

And this particular story, told to me when I needed it most, did exactly that. It was a catalyst to action, the inspiration I needed to go forward with finishing this book.

Now, think about it—when was the last time you heard a story that inspired you to *do* more, maybe even *be* more? Such a story offers one of those special moments, when it seems that the curtains are pulled aside and there lies before you a grander world than you had ever imagined.

This was the story that was shared with me. And that is the essence of the story I hope to share, throughout this book, with you.

CREA
AND
THE
SUPE
LIFE

PART ONE

CREATIVITY AND THE SUPERHUMAN LIFE

THE SUPERHUMAN EFFECT

INTRODUCTION

Growing up in the Midwest meant that I was going to be exposed to two weather phenomena every year: tornadoes and snow. When the forecast sounded bad, what people feared the most was the unpredictability of the storm path.

Much later, I would learn about something called "the butterfly effect," and it would remind me of those days when my family huddled around the TV wondering how much snow we would have in our neighborhood or, more frighteningly, where a sighted tornado would travel to next.

The butterfly effect, discovered in the 1960s by a meteorology professor at MIT named Edward Lorenz, is the inability to capture the vastness and complexity of large systems of physical phenomena, given the imprecision of human measurement. His studies showed that our deterministic interpretation of the universe is fraught with unpredictability because nature's interdependent cause-and-effect relationships are just too complex to resolve. It also showed that minuscule changes can have massive implications in complex systems because these changes compound as a model progresses.

As Lorenz continued his research into the phenomenon, he began using the example of the flapping of a butterfly's wings as the symbolic representation of tiny changes that, while not creating the typhoon, could alter its trajectory in a weather system.

Our modern culture has popularized and modified the concept of the butterfly effect through movies and books, but the crux is still the same: our world is more sensitive to tiny changes than we often realize.

As are we.

ENTER: THE SUPERHUMAN EFFECT

Our inner being so often longs for something more than what we are met with in life. We want more than average; we want to *be* more than average.

But how do we get there? How do we achieve that? Well, just as Lorenz showed all those many years ago, with tiny changes.

Tiny changes, incremental changes, practiced daily—on purpose—can, like the flap of those butterfly wings, grow and expand into much more. Over time, small changes compound to become big ones. You may be motivated to explore your own life's potential yet feel stymied by how best to go about it. Don't start big. Start small! And then grow into what you want to be.

The right kinds of changes, with repeat practice, become a new way of thinking, a new way of being, even a new way of becoming.

And that's what I've dubbed "the superhuman effect": the way in which tiny steps, taken with thought and care, can over time change our whole lives. Can change us. Can make us into the people we would like to be, excelling at work, excelling at life. Becoming more and more in our lives in every way. Both for ourselves and for others.

WHAT THE SUPERHUMAN EFFECT IS NOT

The superhuman effect is not a fad. It is not a self-motivation formula, promoted purely for the sake of self-improvement. The superhuman effect says, *I am determined to go after a life that is great for me and simultaneously improves the lives of others around me.*

There is plenty of material out there that can help us grow as individuals simply for the purpose of improving our own daily lives or finding our passion in life. I love much of this material because some of the principles do give us insights into important areas of life such as relationships, careers, and wellness. But the key to the superhuman effect lies in not only being better in our own lives but also being greater, because so many other people in our lives *need us* to be greater. Even if we can identify only one person in our lives whom we deeply care about, we are implicitly or explicitly asked to be more for their sake.

Becoming superhuman, in the terms I'm talking about, extends beyond self-improvement for self-improvement's sake. It is more about how our search to discover our full potential improves the circles we move in, improving life not only for ourselves but for others as well. Recognizing that we can do this in an organization with the people we work with and even beyond, in all areas of our life, is an exciting aspect of the superhuman life. Living "superhuman-by-design" means that you are aware of your impact on the world around you and that you'll work hard not to forget it when life's journey places difficulties and challenges in your path.

Another important note to remember: the superhuman effect is not built purely on individual talent. While it is an important part of pushing our creativity to new levels, talent alone will not fuel our superhuman journey. Talent is celebrated in our culture, but it is not the only foundation to build on and to rely on if you want to accomplish more. In fact, while talent can be a great starting point, building a foundation for life on talent alone can actually hold you back from pursuing endeavors that will have greater impact in your life. I have discovered that by focusing solely on talent, we can miss the opportunity to have reach and impact in other areas of our lives.

Take a moment to think about well-known athletes, celebrities, and actors who were great in their profession and then demonstrated the ability to be successful in a completely different industry or arena, such as politics, broadcasting, or business ownership. Names that come to mind include Lisa Leslie, who went from being one of the greatest basketball players in history to being a co-owner of the Los Angeles Sparks WNBA franchise, or Michael Strahan, who, after playing fifteen seasons in the NFL, became a well-known and celebrated cohost and broadcaster. Though they were talented in the focus of their original profession, these athletes extended those abilities and their efforts to grow into new areas, so as to make life richer and fuller for others. It wasn't talent alone that drove them. We also see this with everyday people who did not start out in the limelight. These are the individuals who were already leading successful careers and then continued to evolve by engaging their creativity in new ways to do even more in their lives. One of my favorite examples is Ken Jeong, who was already a successful physician before becoming a breakout star in a number of Hollywood movies and sitcoms.

Though it might be obvious, I think it warrants saying that our individual talent is just one of the elements that unlock the doors to pursuing our potential. As I share more about my superhuman-by-design story, my hope for you is that you will see the amazing things you already have inside and then grow quickly to see that you can be and do so much more.

So, with that, let's prepare to put on our capes and take the leap of faith into a journey that will inspire others!

WHY SUPERHUMANS LIVE BY DESIGN

These days I hear a lot about "superpowers." That's not just a generalization—it's an observation. As a creative professional who has worked at several tech organizations in Silicon Valley, California, I have noticed that a favorite first-round interview question is "What's your superpower?"

When most people think of superpowers, what comes to mind is something they saw in a movie, usually one of those Marvel blockbusters with big special effects and an epic score. But while we may thrill to stories about superpowers, what most of us really want in our own lives is the ability to be our greatest selves. I call that the ability to be *superhuman*.

WHY WE LOVE SUPERHUMANS

The prefix *super* means over and beyond. When I speak of being "superhuman," I mean living in a way that exceeds the normal, average expectations of your everyday life. I mean wanting more, striving for more. Striving for excellence and virtue in all areas of your life. Striving to live up to your fullest potential as a human being. Striving always, seeking always, to become everything you can be. This means achieving more on a professional level, in your work life. It also means achieving greater depth and fulfillment in your personal life. It means being more for you yourself as well as for those in your life.

I know, I know—that sounds like a lot. But what if I told you that the path to living a superhuman life is 100 percent within your control? Not sure you can do it?

Don't worry—I used to think the same thing. That is why we are going to walk through this big idea together.

FICTIONAL SUPERHEROES AND REAL-LIFE SUPERHUMANS

Let's start with the concept of a "hero." We love heroes. All of us have grown up hearing some sort of story about heroes, no matter our origin or culture. Of course, some are real and some are mythical, but, arguably, they share certain definable characteristics. To my mind, two of those characteristics are the willingness to sacrifice and the moral desire to do something good for humanity. In that, I'm right in line with the American scholar Joseph Campbell, author of *The Hero with a Thousand Faces.* For Campbell, a hero is someone

> ***who has found or done something beyond the normal range of achievement and experience. A hero is someone who has given his or her life to something bigger than oneself.***

Campbell's conception of the hero has been widely accepted, and he had a good deal more to say about heroes and their work. But this sums up the crux of it.

So we've accounted for the "hero" portion of the equation. But what about the "super" part? Psychologist Robin S. Rosenberg and comics scholar Peter Coogan, who have studied superheroes extensively, acquiesce to Campbell's conception and build on it further:

> ***The super part indicates powers or abilities that are significantly greater than those of the average person (though they need not be "beyond those of mortal men" or women).***

The American comic-book writer and editor Danny Fingeroth, who has also made the study of superheroes a part of his work, says that they share

> ***some sort of strength of character (though it may be buried), some system of (generally-thought-to-be) positive values, and a determination to, no matter what, protect those values. . . The superhero—more than even the ordinary fictional hero—has to represent the values of the society that produces him.***

In other words, being a hero, whether in fiction or in fact, is already a big deal because the hero is selfless for the sake of a larger cause. They are doing more than the average person in the most consequential of moments. To be categorized, on top of that, as "super" is about making the canvas even bigger and bolder. Not only do superheroes devote their lives to a greater mission, but also their character exemplifies the best values of the society they serve. The superhero is typically depicted as championing the highest standards and upholding the most virtuous codes. Superheroes possess a mindset that is mission-oriented and prosocial: they strive to lead a life filled with meaning and intentional purpose not only for themselves but also for the greater community they are connected to.

All right, this is getting fun—we now have the beginning of a shared understanding of the word *superhero* and how the superhero genre reflects on the human condition. Throughout the book, I will continue to give you inspirational examples of superheroes as the apex of the hero narrative. Superheroes appeal to our inner aspiration to *do* and to *be* more. To do the heroic thing when called on and to be something greater for ourselves and for others around us. They also speak to our longing to commit to a cause greater than ourselves, to leverage our abilities to live a life that inspires others and represents the societal traits we value the most—things like integrity, honesty, and bravery. Superhero stories have kept billions of comic fans engaged and wanting more over the decades, and in more recent years, they have become one of the most successful genres in Hollywood.

Need proof? The Marvel Studios movies *Avengers: Infinity War* in 2018 and *Avengers: Endgame* in 2019 each surpassed $2 billion in worldwide grosses. As this book goes out in the world, the Marvel Cinematic Universe ranks as the highest-grossing film series of all time.

So, with all of the money and success coming from the superhero genre, there must be something else—something beyond being heroic and mission-oriented, something beyond being a reflection of our aspirations—that draws us to superheroes so strongly. Rosenberg has spent years studying superheroes and our relationship to them. She says that superheroes provide us with escape, that their familiar story lines are comforting, that they provide us with someone to root for, and that they allow us to see our own problems, even existential crises, worked out on an epic scale. She also makes the point that superheroes are at once like and not like us. She observes that their most distinguishing feature, their superpowers,

> ***can make us fantasize what it would be like to be them, while at the same time wishing there were someone who was like them in real life.***

There is something, along with everything else, thrilling about those superpowers!

Whether kids or adults, we respond to those superheroic tales. And part and parcel of that superheroism are the superpowers, which have fascinated generations of fans. Perhaps they have fascinated you as well? For my part, I've always been particularly drawn to superheroes who possess all the requisite attributes of being "super"—that is, they have powers beyond those of mortal men and women and yet are themselves mortal, or human, as opposed to alien. These are superheroes who have particularly earned the right to be called "super."

Take Batman, for example. Unlike Superman, who was seen as an alien from another planet, Batman is depicted as a regular human being whose personal drive, rigorous mental and physical wellness, and intense focus allowed him to achieve superhuman powers. He's not the only mortal to gain such status, of course. Spider-Man, for example, is a regular mortal, or at least he started out that way. However, his superpowers did not come entirely from his own efforts, but rather from developing the strengths of his newfound abilities, which were granted him in the form of a bite from a radioactive spider. Both superheroes' stories are inspirational tales of mortal beings who achieve great things through their own efforts. But Peter Parker (Spider-Man) got a physical boost from that spider bite. Bruce Wayne (Batman) did it despite having the body of a regular mortal with no special powers.

Though characters from all manner of superhero universes can inspire and inform, the term *superhuman* as I use it is derived from those superheroes who began as regular humans and who then gained extraordinary powers and abilities, either by creating something positive out of a woeful circumstance or by applying a new mindset to their life journey. They're not superheroes who were born with superpowers and extraordinary talents and gifts; they are instead humans who, over time, transformed themselves into superhumans.

In real life, I have met gifted and talented people who have repeatedly exhibited superheroic character in their lives. Such people show us through their actions that what we believed to be impossible can be achieved. They show us that we can leverage our own strengths to do the same. And they show us that we can achieve incredible results, both professionally and privately, all while living a life that many people find commendable and inspirational. As I started to list the superhumans I have met in my life and the ones I admire from afar, two questions quickly followed: How have they done this? And can everyone live out, in a similar fashion, their own superhuman journey?

TOWARD THE SUPERHUMAN

Superhumans think in terms of how extensively they can impact the world for a greater cause. As they journey through their lives, they become more and more convinced that *all* citizens of the world can work collaboratively to create a better world. Superhumans are not new. We have seen them over and over again throughout history. We've read about their legacies in history and literature. But we are especially aware of them in the Internet era, when information and experiences are shared faster than ever before.

Are these people fundamentally different? Or have they tapped into something that has enabled them to grow?

I believe the latter. I believe that we can all make that journey—and that we should, if we feel impelled or called to do so. If we want that better, larger life. We have the choice to be mindful about living to our full potential and to devote ourselves to doing so, not just for ourselves, but for those around us. Every day we are presented with opportunities to develop our own abilities. Each day offers us the chance to move beyond the things that often hold us back from our dreams—our insecurities, our internal doubts, and our fears—in order to build a life that is not only fulfilling but also memorable.

Our emphasis, then, must be on developing the elements of what makes each of us special to the world: our own "superpowers." When we talk about the idea of having superpowers, what we really mean is leveraging our gifts and talents to live an extraordinary life filled with extraordinary, life-changing moments. If you're laser-focused on leveraging these gifts and talents, you will recognize that you need more than motivation to achieve life-changing outcomes that matter. You also need to be able to tap into your natural abilities consistently. The superhumans of the world understand that what they already carry within them is only the starting point and that other factors come into play as they strive to live to their fullest potential.

As I started to work on growing my own superpowers, and on developing a way to consistently leverage those powers, I quickly realized how important codifying my values would be if I also wanted to be radically more effective in the world. From there, I needed to figure out how to live this new idea, and then how to make it relatable to many others. The superhuman life is one inspired by the mythical and the real, a life that answers some of the deepest yearnings we all have. It is a life that beckons us to awaken the most creative parts of our being so as to amplify the uniqueness of our nature, all in an effort to extend beyond the average and the mundane. But how do we live as superhumans? How do we boldly embark on a journey that invites us to *do* more and to *be* more, all while representing the highest values of our society and humanity?

And the answer to that question was "by design." Let's take a closer look at what that means.

THE DESIGN APPROACH TO CREATING CHANGE

As a designer, I absolutely love the fact that the word *design* is now a household word. I believe that the cause-and-effect relationships between new technology and our consumer demands have brought a heightened sensibility to the topic of design over the past decade.

At the heart of design is the human ability to work creatively and imagine new solutions to a problem. *Design* is both a noun and a verb. Think of creativity as the core of design (the noun), and of design (the verb) as the process we exercise to arrive at a potential desired outcome. The outer shell is Design with a capital "D" because it represents the product, service, and/or experience that we interact with as consumers. In the case of product design (my specialty), this is often the exciting and aesthetically appealing object that you take out of the package and weave into your daily life and habits.

When I use the word *design* as a verb, it is a word of action. Using *design* as a noun puts the emphasis on the result—that is, on Design with a capital "D" (as in "Oh, what a beautiful Design. . ."). What customers typically experience as the final Design is really the accumulation of lots of micro designs and iterations along the path to producing an outcome that we can interact with on a sensory level.

Working as a designer, I've seen this process in action. I've seen it work, time and again, and I'd like to share those insights with you. I want you to see how this process, one filled with an abundance of curiosity and iteration, can be used to grow and deepen your own creativity and ultimately yield results that you could never have imagined. It is "by design" that designers intentionally build things that don't yet exist in the world to meet the needs, desires, and requirements of themselves and others. And it will be "by design" that you and I do the same thing in our lives.

DESIGNING BY DOING

When I am working on a project requiring my design expertise, I am designing by taking action. For instance, a designer will typically create a prototype:

generate early samples, models, or releases of a product to evaluate use cases, validate assumptions, and test ideas. The key activities in this process are often described under the rubric *design thinking*. I am sure some of you have heard of design thinking before, and perhaps you even leverage it in your workday.

At its heart, design thinking is an intentional, iterative, and collaborative process that seeks to understand the audience using the product, that reframes problems in terms of this audience, and that is inclined toward actions like prototyping—all in order to create innovative solutions for the marketplace. The design-thinking process, which is now taught in organizations all over the world, is typically described as having four phases: Empathize, Define, Ideate, and Test. A helpful mnemonic for remembering these phases is "EDIT." The acronym is particularly apt as it reminds us that this process entails constantly refining, modifying, and improving something.

I leveraged this process in client projects during my time at IDEO, a global design firm founded in 1991 in Palo Alto, California. IDEO is one of the most successful and written-about global design agencies in the world, with a track record of creating useful products that goes all the way back to Apple's computer mouse. When I joined the firm in 2012, one of my favorite design books was *Change by Design*, by the president and CEO of IDEO at the time, Tim Brown. In that book, Brown explains that so much work in the design profession consists of designing by doing:

> ***Design thinking requires bridging the "knowing-doing gap." The tools of the design thinker—getting out into the world to be inspired by people, using prototyping to learn with our hands, creating stories to share our ideas, joining forces with people from other disciplines—are ways of deepening what we know and widening the impact of what we do.***

This emphasis on action helped me evolve quickly as a designer. Designing by doing helped me figure out ways to imagine and then create novel, patentable concepts. Even more, IDEO showed me that while there was no method for predicting the future response to a solution—or even for predicting whether we would arrive at a solution—there is a process for making the experience repeatable and enriching for all. Designing by doing became so valuable in my work DNA that it began influencing my perspective away from the studio as well.

LIVING WITH INTENTION IS LIVING BY DESIGN

As I was working to shape outcomes to achieve my own goals, I realized that I could extend the design-thinking approach into my private life.

Doing something *by design* meant being strategic, purposeful, intentional, and as thoughtful as possible about what I hoped to be and what I hoped to accomplish. It also meant leveraging certain phases of the design-thinking process to help me grow my potential by being as creative-minded as I could. Furthermore, when external challenges made it difficult to reach my goals, I would no longer be at a loss for how to break through. Now I would approach these challenges and overcome resistance to forward progress *by design*.

Through the superhuman-by-design journey, I believe that anyone can maximize their full potential and alter the trajectory of their lives. Since the core of the design process is creativity, we will now look at how being strategically invested in developing our creative selves is the foundation of living superhuman.

Don't think you are that creative?

Well, let's punctuate this chapter with an encouraging thought from IDEO partner Tom Kelley:

> ***We all have a creative side, and it can flourish if you spawn a culture to encourage it, one that embraces risks and wild ideas and tolerates the occasional failure.***

To understand how to cultivate your creative side, one full of curiosity and fresh perspective, we will first look at the 3 C's of Creativity.

THE THREE C'S OF CREATIVITY

The first step along the path to living a superhuman life is to break down the invisible walls that hinder your creativity. But before you take that step, it's helpful to understand the value of creativity and why it's so integral to becoming superhuman.

As with anything worth achieving, becoming superhuman requires a process. It is a new paradigm, a growth mindset, that we undertake to instill and nurture—by design. When we say we are doing something "by design," we mean that we're taking strategic, intentional action. By design, we will explore our most creative character traits, talents, and gifts with the intention of using these inherent characteristics to systematically reveal, and then pursue, new levels of potential in our daily lives.

THE IMPORTANCE OF CREATIVITY

The core of all design is creativity. Without creativity, there is no motivation to drive the intentional decisions and problem-solving required by the design-thinking process—and there are no insights to draw upon either. By creativity, I mean the deeply inventive and imaginative aspects we feel inspired by. Creativity is about finding and applying original ideas, with the hope of generating new solutions. Creativity springs up for all of us at one time or another. We have all experienced being creative, perhaps by bringing an idea to life or approaching a problem differently. But creativity can be an elusive thing. How do we summon it when we want? How do we ensure that we are creative all the time?

It took me years to turn creativity into a daily practice. For a while, I felt that only certain people were creative. I even thought of my own creativity dismissively, often feeling that my sketching and free thinking (two techniques I employ) were something to be kept in check. But through my design work, I discovered that practicing how to think creatively led to incredible results in my projects. During my first design internship, at Coca-Cola North America in Atlanta, Georgia, I noticed that the more creative I was, the more meetings I was invited to join. Coca-Cola impressed on me that novel ideas are introduced and built on by creative thinkers. Often these ideas would lead to memorable and celebrated brand campaigns viewed by millions worldwide.

But it was my time at IDEO that radically expanded my view of creativity and revealed not only that creativity could be practiced, but also that everyone could be creative. The key to IDEO's impressive portfolio of solutions is to make sure that everyone feels like an important participant throughout the creative process of a client project. While with the company, I watched as the studio leads conducted brainstorms, or creative group discussions, with the intention of getting the entire room to generate new ways of solving problems.

Brainstorming is one of the most popular and successful techniques for helping people reach into themselves and feel empowered to freely introduce new ideas. IDEO relies on brainstorming to give people a safe and communal environment in which to solve complex problems. Their brainstorming sessions are not meant to highlight an exact solution or path, but rather to unleash everyone's creative thinking, to stimulate their ability to imagine things from fresh perspectives and to envision possibilities that may not be apparent in any other context. I saw firsthand that these group sessions often became ground zero for innovation. Professionals from various disciplines and business verticals would often enter the brainstorming session convinced that they would produce nothing and that they were not creative. But within an hour, the walls would be covered with Post-It Notes, full of ideas, quick sketches, and diagrams from everyone in the room.

To me, it was magical. Later, when our design team recorded and synthesized the data distributed across the walls, we would sometimes add pictures, sketches, or additional notes for categorizing the comments. From these sessions, our teams would continue the design process, and then weeks later, with the addition of research and prototyping, we'd arrive at solutions that were novel and unique and that, more often than not, impressed our clients. What I gained at IDEO was experience with this practice of effectively exploring a range of perspectives and ideas. I also realized that my best contributions to the room came from being as original as possible and leading imaginatively with ideas that were grounded and energetic and that could be built on by others. Then I thought, *what if I could bring this level of creativity to other areas of my life besides design?*

Fast-forward years later and I am still engaging each day with as much of my creative self as possible. Thinking creatively is my starting point before applying the lens of design to focus my attention and energy on the outcomes I want. After working in the trenches of hundreds of design projects over the past decade—and seeing many adopt the design-thinking process fruitfully—I am convinced that you can be creative as well. I am also convinced that being your best creative self puts you on the path of a superhuman-by-design life.

Now, to plug into our most creative selves and master the art of cultivating creativity, we will look at what I call the *3 C's of Creativity*: consciousness, connection, and community. Once we've done that, you'll see more clearly how a creative life is an inspired life, and how, when guided by design, a focused and purposeful creativity can alter and transform your experiences, both at work and at home.

The three attributes work together closely. The core of our creative self begins with consciousness. As we expand our network and grow our relationships, we begin orbiting in the realm of connection. Finally, our community represents the ecosystem that we inspire, influence, and make an impact in. The ever-expanding nature of the 3 C's means that our tiny, daily changes toward being and living superhuman-by-design can have a huge ripple effect down the line.

THE FIRST "C": CONSCIOUSNESS

Neuroscientists tell us that the mind is "plastic." In other words, by changing our habits and behaviors, we can actually retrain our brain to better cope with the challenges that life throws in our path every day. We can learn to let go of the past, we can choose to ignore unhelpful or negative information, and we can vow to let go of momentary distractions.

By cultivating a mindset that overturns mental barriers and dials down immediate distractions, we can produce a conscious state that enables us to focus on the specific opportunities in front of us. This isn't to say that there won't be other external circumstances demanding our attention, but we can learn to quiet our minds and focus on what's truly important. We will look at examples of some of these activities in Part Two of this book.

Being present and conscious shows us that we are on the path to becoming superhuman because we are mastering our operations of thought. Staying conscious not only produces a greater self-control and equanimity but also allows us to see more clearly a range of possible ideas and how to connect them to forge a new solution. When we are conscious, we are acutely aware of what influential people are sharing with us and aware of our surroundings. Despite whatever may be preoccupying us in the back of our minds, our creativity benefits from our remaining conscious of our environment, our goals, and our endeavors—and also of the people in our lives who matter most.

Consciousness is about training our minds as much as possible to be in the "now" and to be awakened to our own thoughts as well as to the world around us. The greatest athletes seem to be able to do this in the highest-pressure situations. Whether professional, Olympic, or collegiate, athletes at the top of their game sense every single aspect and element of the moment in order to prepare themselves to deliver extraordinary results. An example from a different area of expertise is surgeons' ability to stay present and in the moment for hours on end. Often, they are on their feet for operations that can span several hours. Without their extreme consciousness and concentration, many lives would be lost. To engage our creative selves, we can start by experimenting with practices that help us become more conscious of the world around us, the conversations we have with others, and the work we set out to accomplish each day.

THE SECOND "C": CONNECTION

Connection is one of the fundamental elements of opening new creative pathways in your life. Our ability to learn how to connect produces tremendous value both in our lives and in the lives of others as we become superhuman. Some of the world's most renowned leadership experts acknowledge that our learned ability to connect with people is critical to our developmental journey. John C. Maxwell, who has written dozens of well-regarded books on how people communicate, puts it this way:

> ***You will only be able to reach your potential—regardless of your profession or chosen path—when you learn to connect with other people.***

Whether meeting one on one, in a small team, or with a larger audience, I have trained myself to be conscious of the effort I am putting into connecting with people.

First, let's look at the importance of connecting with others. People who have unlocked their creative selves and have begun to operate as superhumans have learned to maximize their presence in the moment and to connect to the hearts and minds of those around them. Superhumans exercise methods to stay as present as possible with the goal of listening and learning about the value people bring to a conversation. The more conscious I am of the potential that a connection with another person can open, the more curious I am about their interests, aspirations, and philosophies. Ultimately, I am paying attention to how I am responding to the person and doing my best to keep a mindset focused on giving them my most thoughtful and receptive attitude. It takes a lot energy, and I don't always get it right. But in the end, it is worth it to put conscious, intentional effort into making connections with people.

But why put so much energy into going beyond networking in a professional context, even if it means just having a casual conversation with an individual at a meetup?

Because some of the most innovative and positive results in any field are driven by people who figure out ways to connect. By connecting with others, we can transcend the bias and unconscious barriers that keep us from understanding each other's proposals and ideals. Connecting with others leads to collaboration, and through collaboration we come to understand a variety of unique and diverse perspectives, which in turn can produce dynamic results in the workplace and rewarding changes in our personal lives, our homes, and the community. We see it every year in some capacity. We can observe asynchronous and synchronous teams connecting physically and virtually, working hard to collaborate and resolve a crisis or to bring about some monumental change in a decaying system through new solutions.

As I complete this book, the world is experiencing a global pandemic unlike anything that has been seen for at least a century. The novel coronavirus (COVID-19) has claimed nearly a million lives so far, and the number of deaths continues to climb. Scientists, researchers, and many renowned teams in various fields of medicine are progressing at speeds like never before to get a vaccine to stage-one clinical trials. One scientist and viral immunologist, Dr. Kizzmekia Corbett, a young Black woman who is leading the charge to develop a vaccine for COVID-19 at the National Institutes of Health, is collaborating with teams around the world to move the process forward as quickly as possible. The pressure of connecting the dots so rapidly is palpable, but if they are successful, they will change the world. Corbett's work is an example of how connecting with others can lead to potentially rich collaborative experiences that, in turn, can yield amazing results.

In my own experience, I have come to see that as I practice being conscious of my outlook on the world and of my emotions, I can practice the tools that foster meaningful connections with people. Over time, as I have leveraged tools that build connections, I have been able to see growth in my own productivity and influence on others. Through my time at IDEO, I saw how connecting with others enabled our design teams to work together better while also discovering the solutions that impressed our clients. Connecting with others paved the way for us to effect change in clients' organizations and helped us tell objective stories of the value we brought to each project.

When individuals on a team connect with each other, they spend time going beyond their own assumptions and gaining a richer understanding of the perspectives of others. When a person tries to understand the perspectives of others, they have started down a path of empathy, one that leads colleagues to a shared understanding of experiences. As superhumans, we can design for moments like these in our communities as well, by becoming active in local school boards and community-focused groups. As I have participated in more community forums discussing topics such as education and voting, I have gained an expansive perspective that has allowed me to more deeply relate to and care about other people.

Connection requires us to take action. This move to action encourages all of us to think about more than just our own ideas and solutions. It is an unselfish mindset that frees us from the typical insecurities that we all have when focusing only on our own perspectives or ideas.

Connection can also mean remaining open to opportunities to enrich our own understanding of who we are and who we are becoming. Initially, I thought connecting with myself meant evaluating my own progress or productivity. Years later, I realized that this is a narrow point of view that discouraged me from going deeper. I started taking the time to question my own motivations, interests, and biases. I also began to practice giving and asking for constructive feedback. With this feedback from my peers, I could develop ways to improve my character and strengthen my shortcomings.

That is exactly where the creativity really started to kick in. I was now able to approach growth from a healthier, more confident perspective. Now, when I feel resistance to believing in what I have to offer on a project, at home, or with friends, I intentionally engage in an iterative activity to help me reconnect with my internal sources of renewal. By connecting with the raw expressions of my creative core, I am able to approach my life with purpose, strategy, and intention. I believe you can as well, and in Part Two of this book we will explore ways that you can do this.

Connecting with Your Creative Core

I am convinced that the more you connect with your creative core—that is, your innate creativity—the more impactful your contributions to the world will become for others, especially those who matter to you the most. In order to maximize your full potential and be the best version of yourself, you must learn how to connect with your spirit, mind, and body—all with the goal of managing whatever may be resisting your creative thoughts on how to approach personal growth and development.

In every creative brainstorming session that I run, I give permission to the roomful of people to be as imaginative and wild with their thoughts and ideas as possible. No idea is discouraged. This encourages people to connect with their innate creativity and to think about and even visualize new solutions. In fact, here's the best news I can give you, based on the findings of leading researchers in the field: because our creativity is innate, we can tap into it at any time. Tina Seelig, faculty director of the Stanford Technology Ventures Program, has spent many years researching innovation and whether or not we are innately creative. Her takeaway on the notion that only some of us are creative by nature? Pure myth. She puts it this way:

> ***We are all naturally creative and, like every other skill, some people have more natural talent than others. However, everyone can increase his or her creativity, just as everyone can increase his or her musical or athletic ability, with appropriate training and focused practice. We can all learn tools and techniques that enhance creativity, and build environments that foster innovation.***

The universality of creativity—the fact that, with the right tools and training, it's available to all of us—is a theme that will resonate throughout the rest of this book.

Understanding Barriers to Connecting

Connecting with others and with yourself in order to unleash your creativity builds on your daily habit of being conscious about the people and the world around you. If you begin to see the value of connecting, you will work very hard to eliminate the common pitfalls that prevent us from effectively building this practice into our daily lives. These are primarily three:

- → Unconscious bias
- → Personal insecurities
- → Close-minded people

A quick way to sabotage your ability to connect with others is to communicate from a place of bias. Our preconceived notions about someone based on their culture, ethnicity, or even educational background can prevent us from being active listeners to their ideas and proposals. These unconscious biases play out in the back of our minds and prevent us from being curious about the contribution of those around us. When we immediately begin discounting the ideas and creative thoughts of others in the room, we not only remove ourselves from the present moment but can also short-circuit our ability to see new solutions. We all have biases, no matter who we are. Even as a Black man—who is often in a room with others who in addition to the obvious racial difference do not share my cultural experience or heritage—I have learned to be mindful of my biases.

I take intentional, daily action to remain receptive to the creative contributions of others, no matter who they are or where they come from. I am particularly attentive to this in a context where we are all seeking to make more positive contributions to an organization, environment, or product. I recognize that the best idea can come from anyone in the room and that this is the power that superhumans bring to the room. To be our best selves professionally and personally, we must actively go beyond our unconscious biases.

Next, we have to pay attention to how we deal with our personal insecurities.

One of the fastest ways to lose the ability to connect with others—and with your own creative core—is to focus on only your shortcomings.

Think about times when you felt afraid of a new project or some change in your life. Perhaps it was a challenging request at work or a new assignment. Or perhaps you were in a situation with a friend who needed your understanding and support as they battled a major health issue or even the loss of a loved one. More often than not, fear starts and ends with our insecurities. The more time we spend concentrating on why we will not be able to achieve a huge goal or to say the right thing in the moment, the less time we have for offering up original ideas or empathetic, meaningful words. Ultimately, we sabotage our chance to build the deep connections that could lead to new solutions. We also shut down our own personal growth and aptitude for higher emotional intelligence.

So, instead of focusing on our insecurities, we should develop habits that enable us to visualize successfully connecting both with others and with our best creative selves. Think about what you currently do to dispel insecurities. How do you challenge your negative thoughts? What actions do you take when you feel insecure? Do you address these moments through meditation? Through positive self-talk? Through a few minutes of prayer and affirmative thinking? The methods are many, but the goal should be the same: to grow your innate creativity and strengthen your ability to connect, despite any concerns you might have about yourself, the circumstances, or the other people in the room.

Finally, adopt a new attitude about those other people in the room—or in your life. Can they add value for you? Can you add value for them? Can they challenge your ideas? Are you able to challenge their ideas in a constructive way? Connection asks us to make a mental shift in our perspective about the people around us so that we can see the possibilities that everyone brings to the table.

The superhuman life asks us to develop an "everyone can be creative" attitude and then to explore how people in our lives can be powerful allies in achieving our goals. Even more, as we adopt this perspective, we can see how to help them achieve theirs. I am a firm believer that for every problem presented, there is a person who is an answer to that problem. In other words, every problem comes with a person who can help solve it, if you are willing to ask questions and listen to the perspectives of others.

Superhuman people can generate value all the time because they determine how to maximize the people around them in order to shape outcomes toward their goals. Although being open-minded to others and their ideas may initially seem daunting, adopting an attitude that helps you see the value that people bring to the table will foster stronger connections and will keep you curious about new and unique solutions.

THE THIRD "C": COMMUNITY

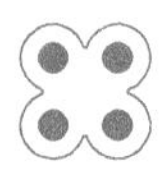

If you are interested in making changes that take you to a better place in your work life and your personal life, then you must first be intentional about connecting with others who are different from you and who also share the desire to take on new challenges. To connect you must also stay conscious of the present moment while keeping an open mind about the bigger world around you. One way that superhumans stay present and begin to act is by connecting to others with a deeper mission and purpose beyond themselves. This is the third element of creativity and activating our creative selves: community.

The greatest superhumans understand that their creativity does not develop in a vacuum. I would argue that even in our most celebrated fictional narratives, we love to see the underdog display extraordinary qualities on their path to achieving audacious goals. In fiction, the path to becoming a superhero is often filled with dramatic, suspenseful, and exciting story lines that are created by the authors to reflect our own aspirations to live to our potential and experience major victories in real life.

Let's take a step back and have some fun with this thought. Think again about that human superhero, Batman.

An odd hero of sorts when compared with other heroes who have superpowers given to them through scientific accidents and freak circumstantial mistakes, Batman is traditionally presented in comic fiction as a man—neither an alien from another planet who was born with superpowers, nor a mutant who was gifted with superpowers. Batman's character and persona are a byproduct of the various communities he searches out or protects in his journey. First, he learns martial arts within a secret community and trains under Ra's al Ghul for twelve years to learn how to master his own mind and overcome his opponents.

Eventually, Batman (known to the public only as Bruce Wayne, billionaire CEO of Wayne Enterprises) leverages the creative gifts of one of his closest allies, Lucius Fox. Batman's collection of weapons, vehicles, and armor secretly comes to life through Fox, who leads the applied sciences division of Wayne Enterprises. Fox and his team provide Batman with a playground of ingenuity and innovation to constantly stay engaged in the latest technology. Soon, he gains access to the very tools he will need to fight crime as a vigilante superhero. Depending on what version of the Batman series you might have followed, Fox even becomes the mastermind behind the design and construction of the Batcave, a top-secret facility hidden beneath Wayne Manor.

When we look at Batman's story, we see how his creativity helps him gain access to a new arsenal of tools and resources. He deliberately sets about connecting with other intelligent, success-oriented people and so builds up a network of allies. Batman even reflects our human tendency to take an ethical stance toward the mission of others by spending just as much time worrying about the city of Gotham and the few good police and the detectives left to protect it.

While Batman's story might offer us a fun and lighthearted reflection on how significant community can be to a superhero's journey, I certainly would not suggest that we view Batman as an example to follow. But perhaps we can look to this character's development for inspiration when it comes to how we see others around us. I have found in my own life that being part of a community means that I have made many connections, all of which can motivate and enhance my natural inventiveness.

In fact, some of the most significant breakthrough moments in my journey to living superhuman occur when I encounter someone who is already much further along on the journey, and their magnetism pulls me in. I am inspired by their very presence, and immediately I am left with a desire to go beyond my mediocrity or stale approach to a problem. In other words, community helps to unlock creative potential.

CREATIVITY IN ACTION: PUTTING IT ALL TOGETHER

Creativity can expand our horizons. Once we have begun the practice of unlocking our creativity so that it can flow into our daily lives, we will also begin to change those lives for the better—*doing* better and *being* better in everything we touch. We must make daily investments in our creative selves in order to begin changing how we approach the opportunities and the challenges we are presented with every day. Becoming superhuman is not an overnight process. It takes time. But if we commit to making positive, intentional steps to transform our approach, the results will show. To illustrate the importance of creativity to the superhuman-by-design life, I want to dive for a moment into my own Silicon Valley story.

The Valley is one of the messiest, most exciting, and most invigorating of all startup environments. There are countless stories of failed ventures and even of fraud and deception among investors and fledgling tech companies. For every success story, there are hundreds of failures. The carnage of failed companies and relationships haunts many founders in the Valley. But the possibility of doing something new and exciting that could potentially also be lucrative beckons, and therefore many of the most talented and entrepreneurially minded people arrive to make their mark and to take a shot at success.

When I started my own company, Forecast Studios, it was initially an attempt to manage the high rents of the Bay Area while searching for a full-time position. With the failure of the first startup I joined, Skully, I had to act fast and leverage my relationships to keep fiscally sound. Nobody could imagine at the time that my small creative team would soon be solving problems for organizations that would affect thousands of people. Our creativity helped us navigate some of the most daunting clients and ultimately helped me see the potential of becoming superhuman in my own daily life.

Breathometer was our first client. The company had gained significant fame through the reality show *Shark Tank* and had even received millions of investment dollars to deliver a new smartphone-enabled digital health device to the market. With fresh investment money on the way, following delivery of their first product, the company was poised to reach the next level with a second health-related quantified-self device.

Initially, our team was hired to produce content marketing for the new product. The small device was about the size of a hockey puck and drew air from inside a person's mouth in order to generate data about the bacteria count. Based on the level of bacteria in the mouth, the device supposedly could supply information about the compounds that could be leading to bad breath or poor oral hygiene. The device also had a companion app that encouraged users to review this information while going through their morning, afternoon, and evening oral hygiene routines.

About three weeks into our contract, we were called into a big, high-stress meeting. At the time, I was acting as both creative director and project manager for the team and had my hands full with the creative work we were already responsible for. But the initial beta devices had been performing poorly with hundreds of test users. As a result, people at the executive level wanted us to redirect our marketing spend from building awareness to somehow solving the retention issue with the device. The app and the device needed to be used together, both for people to maximize its potential in their lives and for Breathometer to collect good data.

This was a moment that demanded game-changing results. The problem had become serious enough that the entire engineering team had shifted their focus to figuring out how to keep people engaged with the device. The meeting room was filled with stressed-out, exhausted engineers who were looking for *any* solution to begin developing.

In this instance, I watched one of my teammates do something that I could never have imagined possible. While the rest of our team sat quietly and listened to the roomful of concerned product people and engineers, my videographer got up and went to the whiteboard on the other side of the room. I was astonished and initially afraid not only that were we going to be fired that day and so lose our first major client, but also that we'd embarrass ourselves in front of the entire leadership team.

But to my surprise and delight, my videographer sketched a solution on the board that completely shifted the atmosphere in the room. He began illustrating cartoon-like characters in a sequence that paralleled a comic book. The illustrations looked like the start to an onboarding animation for the app. Our videographer had devised a way to keep engagement by consolidating multiple steps into simple animations that communicated what a user needed to do in order to get an effective reading from the device. It was absolutely genius.

Not only did we leave the room as heroes, with the rest of the engineering team motivated to implement whatever we designed, but also I was able to negotiate a sizeable change order with the marketing director. We ended up continuing to work with the client, and our influence as well as our budget grew.

How did my videographer achieve this triumph for our team? How did an introverted and reserved member of the Forecast team all of a sudden become the superhuman in the room and deliver a super-successful solution? He had been practicing the 3 C's of Creativity in his daily life, and when the situation called for it, he was ready.

Although some of us come into this world with more creative ability than others, all of us can learn the creative process and leverage it to produce dramatic results. This, of course, does not happen overnight. It takes daily, intentional action to be more creative—in other words, it takes a design process.

In the case of our videographer, he had a deep curiosity about animation and enjoyed illustrating for fun. He had studied film in college. He did not know the first thing about producing an app or designing the user interface/ user experience for the onboarding experience. But every day, he allowed himself a few minutes of extra time to explore his creativity through illustrations of sci-fi characters, often sharing them broadly with his online social media community of artists. His creative ability had become more and more automatic as he followed the practice of daily awareness to pursue something that gave him inspiration. Ultimately, when the moment arrived for him to meet a big challenge, he had already been preparing his superhuman capabilities by practicing simple things in his daily life that strengthened his creative core.

The creative process focuses on what we can do daily in order to build our creative capacity and strengthen our innate creative ability. It is what makes us lifelong learners, and it is what fuels our motivation to develop and improve the skills we need to achieve the successes we are looking for. Pursuing lifelong skills helps to develop and strengthen the characteristics of perseverance, willpower, and self-discipline. These are key ingredients to learning, and are vitally necessary for building on the previous day's progress. When we explore our creativity through learning new perspectives, processes, and tools, we are designing a life that supports experimentation and rewards the generation of new ideas.

Thus, living superhuman happens when you take your ability to become "creative on command"—that is, more predictably creative—and then design the conditions to grow it, support it, and invite it. This by-design creativity is a process anyone can learn. I call it the iterative journey.

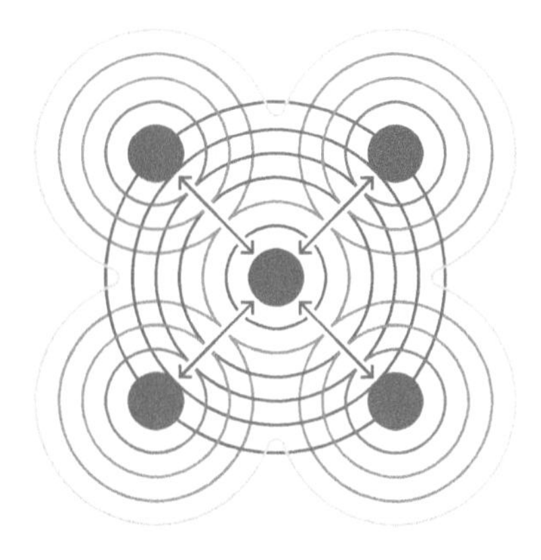

● Consciousness

THE ITERATIVE JOURNEY

The iterative journey can be understood as the daily steps we can all take to put our creativity into action. If creativity is the heart of living superhuman, then iteration is the process we adopt to live it *by design*. In other words, it is the process of dynamic trial and error by which we grow into our maximum potential.

Engaging and growing your creative core requires building elements into your life that support and reinforce your innate—that is, your natural and inborn—creative abilities. There are already hundreds of automatic actions you engage in every day, many subconsciously. With iterative practice, creativity too will become automatic. However, to begin with, for many of us, engaging our creative self can become an obstacle because we notice the barriers that prevent us from sorting through and capitalizing on our most innovative and unconventional solutions.

But there's hope! Just as is the case when cultivating any new habit as part of your daily practice, growing your creative behavior can become a new way of engaging your mind despite the daily distractions of life. You won't always get it right. I don't always get it right. In fact, that is the point of developing a daily practice, and that is the point, too, of investigating new avenues. Make a plan to explore different environments, tools, and communities to learn what helps you be more imaginative. Sometimes an activity I try inspires me to express myself differently or to come up with something new. And sometimes it doesn't. What matters most is being intentional, purposeful, and deliberate about inviting opportunities into your life that help you be more creative on demand.

When I teach new designers the design process, I can see that they are keen to be more creative with their work, but that they simply do not know how to begin, how to nurture and grow that creativity. By engaging in the process, they can reliably generate innovative solutions, which can, in turn, lead to extraordinary results. Through this process, they can in time reach their full potential as innovative thinkers.

MIRRORING THE DESIGN PROCESS

The major obstacle to developing a deeper level of creativity within yourself is often in discovering how to gain new perspectives in specific areas of your life. The design process can usher in such new perspectives. Remember, the process is typically described by four phases: Empathize, Define, Ideate, and Test. You can recall these phases with the acronym EDIT.

Empathizing

The first phase of the design process involves in-depth research to better understand a particular person's or group's needs. This phase is typically called the Empathizing phase because it is about pushing aside personal assumptions or bias and becoming deeply curious in order to gain insights on intrinsic needs that a user or group of users might have as they relate to an experience. For instance, designers might research what a better shopping experience could be like for customers at a store. During this research phase, a design team might spend time observing the most challenging moments of a shopping experience and listening to users' own descriptions of those experiences, with the hope of discovering potential areas in which to improve the customer experience.

The superhuman-by-design version of this design step mirrors the goal of gaining as much insight as possible when making decisions about your life. Empathy in a superhuman's life is about being self-aware, open-minded, and conscious of both the world around us and our own interior world. To exercise this observation in service of growing and strengthening my creative core, I continually look for ways to better understand the perspectives of other people. It requires a lot of attention and energy, but it also means that I am lowering my ego and listening to their opinions on spiritual matters, finances, business, health, and work relationships. I also pay attention to the environments and habits that nurture my creativity. For instance, I find that listening to a podcast about the journeys of successful entrepreneurs broadens my perspective and helps me gain valuable insights about their experience. My understanding of different cultures often comes by practicing a few words in another language with a person who is fluent in that language.

Defining

The second phase of the design process builds on the first to define the needs that the design team will be solving for. The Defining phase of the design process thus becomes critical to stating the questions and problems a design team must address in the solution. Often design teams spend this time crafting language around the possibilities to be explored later in the process.

In a superhuman's life, the Defining phase can be an ongoing process that encourages us to define the things that help us grow our creativity or identify the obstacles to doing so. I also see this phase as an opportunity to articulate what my superpowers are and how they could be applied to important areas of my life. Now, we have not discussed superpowers much yet—but don't worry, we'll get to them.

For now, consider superpowers as the way to talk about what you do well innately and so what you can be excellent at with more effort and focus over time. In this phase, I will quite simply write down the areas of my life that I have become acutely aware of during the Empathizing phase, and the activities that could potentially help me explore how to go to the next level in these areas. My creativity then becomes the vehicle that helps me think of a variety of possible ways to try out activities and paths that can help me move forward.

Ideating

The third phase of the design process is all about taking action. The Ideating phase focuses on generating new ideas and trying them out through prototyping, or partially implementing ways to try out your ideas. This phase can be the most exhilarating for creative professionals because we get to think outside the box. In the Ideating phase we are challenged to come up with as many ideas as possible and then to evaluate which solutions to try out with inexpensive materials, techniques, and plans. The design process is cyclical, meaning that as superhumans, we will apply this process over and over again with a variety of activities and actions. Personally, I have found that applying this phase of the design process in other key areas of my life is similar to applying it at work on a design problem—and just as fruitful.

For designers, there are a number of visual techniques that promote the generation of and experimentation with new solutions during the Ideating phase. When teaching new designers, I tend to push them through a visual ideation technique called mood boarding that helps them build connections between solutions. In this context, *mood boarding* is the activity of formatting as many ideas, concepts, and thoughts as possible by collecting images and placing them on one canvas—be it physical or digital. But mood boarding goes beyond just finding similar images and building a Pinterest board. More often than not, it is a messy process in which a canvas is filled with rough sketches and inspirational images that have some association with each other. For instance, imagine a canvas filled with images to inform the design of a shoe. The board will be populated with images and sketches that reflect insights based on the information gathered about the target user group, or consumer, in the Empathizing and Defining phases of the design process. Along with rough conceptual renderings, the board might have material samples, merchandising ideas, and even marketing material that hints at how the shoe could be advertised in the marketplace.

The "pinning-up" action of mood boarding can often involve physically placing images on a board or wall that opens the mind to new and unconventional solutions. Though it can be done digitally as well, I often find that the action of sorting and placing images by hand gives me and my colleagues a chance to really see and understand potential connections between the ideas. Sometimes I will cluster images that seem to have a greater association to each other, in the hope that such juxtaposition will spark even more ideas and things to try out.

What is important to understand is that as superhumans we can leverage the actions in this design phase to imagine new ideas, new possibilities, and new solutions for any area of our lives. No matter the topic, we can *ideate*, or form new thoughts, and then choose some of the solutions to try out. We can create environments or opportunities in our lives to prototype these ideas and see how effective they really are. After spending time connecting with people or with my own observations, doing some research, and then defining the area where I want to see growth in my life, I generally move into mood boarding. The action of physically pinning up our new desires, visions, ideals, and aspirations can begin to establish the outcomes we are seeking to accomplish in our lives.

To begin living superhuman lives, we have to keep superhuman possibilities in front of us. As we practice putting up these types of inspiring images, articles, and graphics, we begin to cultivate a habit that is foundational to being creative. During the past few years, I have done this over and over for multiple areas of my life and have seen incredible outcomes. I have tried this with jobs, and I have tried this with wellness.

Even in writing this book, I designed a plan to try out via a board full of Post-Its and images. I plotted out things to experiment with, like creating a brand for the book or starting with only blog posts. I posted photos of where I could imagine my book selling to the public. When it came to the theme of the book, I made a cluster of images of people who were perceived as extraordinary in their lives. For fun, I gathered images of superheroes—fictional women and men—and then found analogous images that answered questions I'd explored in the earlier design phases. For instance, how would a superhuman take care of their body? Would their workout sessions be about maximizing the potential of their body? What actions could I take to examine how very healthy individuals live their daily lives? Eventually, as I explored the aspects of the book through action, I realized that I was generating a cohesive, approachable concept that millions of people could benefit from in their own lives. As we go through the Ideating phase, we will naturally begin to determine what is working for us and what is not.

Testing

The final phase of the design process is the Testing phase. In this phase, designers or even potential end users, such as potential customers, rigorously evaluate the concept produced in the Ideating phase. As the iterative process of design is cyclical, designers will often take the learnings from a prototype and bring those insights and new thinking back into the Defining phase to discuss further refinements. Ultimately, designers want to evaluate whether their solutions are effectively answering their questions and whether their proposals are a great fit for the original needs.

In my life, I find that following this process helps me make the most of my circumstances and what I have at my disposal at any given time. More often than not, we do not have everything we need to ensure that our experience of trying something new is easy and comfortable. But testing can be a way of recording what we learn throughout the process. Through testing in the superhuman life, we have permission to choose the concepts, ideas, and paths that help us rise to another level. Whether I am figuring out a new exercise regimen, a new diet, a new business goal, or even writing my first book, I find that testing helps me see what is working and what is not so that I can pivot quickly to alternative ideas, environments, and solutions.

The Testing phase of the iterative journey also gives us permission to fail. In fact, this phase offers a unique opportunity to figure out what is working and what is not as you pursue your highest potential. This phase of the process can help you get to know yourself more deeply than ever before. Through testing, you have a sense of fulfillment because you will be literally bringing your ideas to life for the purpose of growing as an individual beyond former boundaries. The process of evaluating your short-term changes reflects a humble and maturing internal character, one that sees failures as part of the journey of pushing toward your maximum potential.

Applying the Process in Your Own Life

Through your actions, whether it be a short-term job, a class, or even a networking experience, by working through the design process, you will begin to intuitively understand what is working for you. The last two phases of the iterative journey are the most exciting for superhumans because they generate the most action and because they validate the more intrinsic, thought-provoking steps in the previous design phases. But those earlier phases set the stage for the final ones. They are enormously important. Do not skimp on them.

One important note: I do not require a specific timeline for ideating, prototyping, and testing out my ideas. Rather, I commit to a new activity in approachable chunks that hold me to a time requirement. How do I do this? I choose to explore actions that do not require immediate, drastic life changes and that also tend to have pre-baked timelines associated with them. This can range from trying out a yoga session or guitar lesson on YouTube for twenty minutes a day to using a language-learning app for a few minutes each day for a month. All of these exploratory actions might be in service of a greater goal, such as learning how to communicate better with clients or being able to manage my mental wellness effectively, but they all require a small investment up front.

When I was at Dolby Labs, I was working as one of the creative directors on a new design team. The days were very busy, and I often struggled to reconcile working with taking the time to eat lunch and build relationships. A fellow designer recommended a book from 99U, a design resource from Adobe, called *Manage Your Day-to-Day: Build Your Routine, Find Your Focus, and Sharpen Your Creative Mind*. It was the perfect book at that time because each of the several designers interviewed offered unique perspectives on how they managed their busy days. As I read through the book, I spent time thinking through the feedback from my colleagues, defining the experience I wanted to have during the day at Dolby, and then ideating on ways to maintain my well-being and also build relationships with others at the company.

Finally, I produced a couple of different calendars that encouraged me to try some new ways of approaching my problem. Eventually, I started hosting "lunch and learns"—which gave me an opportunity to share lunch with more people at once and also to connect with newfound colleagues by sharing inspiration. I learned that working closely with the administrator for each marketing VP gave me a chance not only to have lunch with those VPs once or twice a month, but also to get extra presentation time and seed new ideas for big projects that the marketing organization was chartering.

While I have numerous work-related examples, in the end, I discovered that applying the iterative process to all aspects of my life produced tremendous return.

No aspect of your life is too small to rethink and reframe by engaging your most creative self and applying the iterative methodology of design thinking to help you imagine and generate new ideas and solutions.

THE MODEL OF THE SUPERHUMAN

The iterative process is only one aspect of the superhuman-by-design life. The practices of the iterative process establish the habitual steps that help us engage our full potential. As we continue to iterate over the years, we will find what grows our creativity the most and we will move fluidly through the phases as we apply them to our lives. By committing to this cyclical journey, we invite opportunities into our lives that will help us engage our most creative selves.

Putting the iterative process to work will help you identify and grow your superpowers and then sort through different ways of applying those powers to your life. This tried-and-true process produces dramatically positive results for design projects, and it will do the same for you as you awaken and engage your creative core. The 3 C's of Creativity are the foundational elements of creativity, and the iterative journey is the process by which you operationalize them.

I love this process because my failures are already accounted for—in fact, failing in the process gives me more insight that I can then revisit through another round of ideation. So now, when someone tells you to "think outside the box," you have not only a process for doing that but also a practice that is firmly a part of your superhuman life!

The iterative process becomes effective only when you embrace the idea that your innate creative ability can open the door to scores of possibilities. It sounds simple, but it is profoundly true that as we think, so we are. Even the most spontaneous actions that seem to spring from our unconscious minds are driven by whatever thoughts we embrace most firmly. If we believe in our innate creative ability, and if we believe that we can gain other life-changing powers through our own agency, we can build superhuman lives with the design process. As you begin the journey of living life to the fullest, you will see that the creative self, as developed by application of the design process, is wonderfully effective. Your life will change for the better.

But living life to the fullest also means that we commit to a higher purpose, and more often than not, even a higher mission. I want to emphasize that living superhuman-by-design is not just about success, and it is not just about you. When we challenge ourselves to change our condition by becoming superhuman, we must also recognize that our character and values are consequential.

And that's what the Superhuman Code is all about.

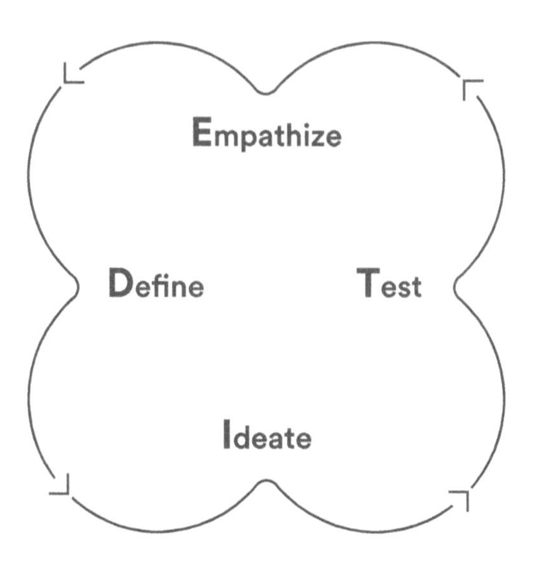
Empathize
Define
Test
Ideate

THE SUPERHUMAN CODE

Contemporary readers of comics know that superheroes tend to represent the "do-gooder," a fictional character filled with good intentions despite the difficulties and grievous implications of the challenges they face. Often, Hollywood chooses the most desirable actresses and actors to play these characters, and they are depicted with polish and beauty.

But there are also lots of characters we can deconstruct who show heroism in a less celebrated package. Can you think of a few less-than-perfect fictional heroes?

How about the Hulk?

Remember the green mutant in the Marvel Universe who can flip cars and take down street poles like dandelions? He is a blockbuster of a character for Marvel. Hulk's alter ego is the soft-spoken and brilliant Dr. Bruce Banner. As a kid, I was always nervous that something was going to set off the normal, human-looking Dr. Banner and cause him to transform into the uncontrollable, vein-popping monster. Rage brought the Hulk on, and rage continued to propel him. Though the Hulk has amazing abilities, he is severely influenced by his emotions. And that causes him and his human counterpart problems.

When I started writing about the superhuman life, I realized that my goal was to detail not only how to leverage creativity and the design process to do more and be more, but also how to do so in the face of adversity. I realized that it was incredibly important to talk about how to craft this lifestyle in the real world, where we constantly face internal challenges, external difficulties, and resistance at all levels in pursuing our endeavors. I wanted to write for an audience looking to manage their lives not only through the most successful moments, but also through the most ugly and regrettable moments.

In my own journey to living superhuman, I discovered how often my emotions could support or plague my efforts to live toward the full measure of my existence. I would often feel triggered by my ups and downs, and I inevitably would act in a way that was uncharacteristic of who I knew I was inside. It was a counterproductive life, one too often driven by my feelings. When I had a great success, I would feel validated, even vindicated, and then proceed to celebrate in ways that would continue to feed my ego. When I failed at a project or felt slighted or even threatened by circumstance, I would respond defensively, often erupting with a passive-aggressive comment or a long email (don't send those, by the way). My response to the highs and lows of life would often put pressure on my overall well-being and ultimately undermine my creative core.

In time, I came to the realization that despite my faith-based moral compass, if I aspired to do more, I needed some superhuman attributes and a value system to build them on.

Though the superheroes I admire vary widely in their powers, abilities, and purposes, they often share one significant characteristic: a guiding code of ethics that influences their reality. Now, I am not going to advocate that we follow the ethical code of a caped crusader, but I *am* going to encourage you to think about the attributes and values that reflect a superhuman character. By "code," I mean guide rails or foundational principles that can govern our conduct and decision-making during both the highs and the lows of life.

The Superhuman Code teaches us that we all have a significant role to play in the world and that we must constantly think beyond ourselves. It is a concept based on understanding that there are ethical principles we can exercise to operate at levels of civic excellence in society. The Superhuman Code is the north star that informs the motivations, goals, and actions of anyone seeking to design a superhuman existence in their lives.

The Superhuman Code is also a reminder that as we focus on achieving a new brand of excellence in our professional and personal lives, we do not seek such results purely for personal success, but also for the positive impact we can have on the lives of others. When we do not honor the principles of the Superhuman Code, we fail to operate at extraordinary levels, and as a result, we miss opportunities to be extraordinary in our daily lives. This is especially the case when we're in the midst of either extreme highs or extreme lows. Without a code of ethics that deepens our character and guides our emotional responses, we become susceptible to ordinary habits and distractions that can produce a life of selfishness, close-mindedness, and mediocrity.

In our pursuit of a superhuman life, our work to grow and develop our creative core must be complemented by our desire to develop character attributes that help us maximize our potential. Guided by the Superhuman Code, we will begin to experience dramatic and dynamic results with respect to our mind and spirit, our health and well-being, our finances, and our relationships—results that exceed our wildest expectations. The goal of being superhuman is to live our life to the fullest potential and to be a positive force in every area of our life in which we interact with other people. And with the Superhuman Code, we can develop the character to help us maintain a superhuman attitude in our life.

THE ATTRIBUTES OF THE SUPERHUMAN CODE

The Superhuman Code has six elements that will grow our mindsets to superhuman levels: awareness, humanity, integrity, humility, resilience, and sacrifice. I have experienced the incredibly positive effects of integrating these attributes into my life over the years. While these six elements might seem an oversimplification, I promise you they are not. Each one is your credential, and each builds on the others. No matter your personality type or the circumstances you are facing, these elements will serve you well as you imagine new horizons in your life and create a richer and more meaningful experience for yourself and others.

Awareness

Know yourself. How many times have you heard this maxim? And how true it is. The consciousness needed to build your innate creative muscles begins with your individual sense of awareness. When I speak of "awareness," I am specifically referring to becoming cognizant of how your thoughts, your beliefs, and your internal dialogue affect both your private and your public life.

Awareness is necessary for several reasons, and like any other attribute, must be managed as much as possible. For instance, if we have a heightened sense of public self-awareness, we might be overly concerned with whether and in what way others are judging us and our actions. By contrast, if we are focused excessively in the other direction—that is, on ourselves—we can become deeply conceited. A balanced sense of awareness can be a positive influence in your life. A balanced and healthy awareness supports us in three ways.

Awareness builds a growth mindset. The growth mindset depends on our recognizing that learning is a lifelong endeavor and that our journey of living superhuman does not end until we leave this earth. As we become more aware of behaviors that have served us poorly or problems that we want to solve, attuning our individual awareness to these conditions can help us consciously seek solutions. Even more, as we strengthen our awareness, we can pick up more signals and gain a higher level of consciousness about the connections and communities that yield positive outcomes. In this way, awareness invites us to embrace what we don't know and encourages us to improve through development. I have personally seen how self-awareness challenges me to logically evaluate how I am "showing up" and then becomes the initial spark to further personal growth. The more we embrace a growth mindset, the more we are able to shape our outcomes toward the hopes and aspirations we discover for areas of our lives in the early design phases.

Awareness helps us be more human (than robot). One of my favorite books that address the ways in which our individual awareness can affect others is *There Is No Good Card for This*, by Kelsey Crowe, a professor of social work and a breast cancer survivor, and Emily McDowell, the creator of a greeting-card line called Empathy Cards. The authors make the point that

> ***when you recognize that bad things happen to good people, and also, that bad things actually happen to you—it creates a connection around suffering that is a two-way relationship between equals.***

This recognition is paramount because unless you can develop an awareness of how your highs and lows in life fuel a larger purpose, you are bound to live an existence disconnected from others. In the moment, this is difficult to do and to act on, and I still do not always get it right—but in striving for the superhuman life, I practice having an awareness of what others around me are feeling and how my behavior affects their actions. Often this comes by way of listening deeply to the goals and challenges of other people before responding. This helps me behave empathetically, as I've now seen things from their perspective. In turn, I am able to move past the starting point of positive intent and become more fully aware of how to have a positive impact.

Awareness helps you see what's holding you back. As in the design process, research helps us uncover our own blind spots, biases, and limiting beliefs. Much of this research involves awareness of our ability to ask questions, seek advice, and listen to the counsel of others. This awareness is the credential we need to suspend that unguarded trust in our own abilities to navigate big choices all by ourselves, to evaluate the consequences and implications of our decisions, and ultimately to discover and draw on the best creative solutions for our growth.

Humanity

Our obsession with maintaining youth, our drive to live as long as possible, our struggles to rebound from challenging circumstances, the wrestling we do, from time to time, with our purpose in life—these are all examples of how we engage our humanity. Humanity is the spirit that infuses such questions directly related to existence, and our awareness of it often shapes our greater purpose and the influence we have in the lives of others.

While the DC Comics superhero Batman always stood out for me as a fictional superhuman who was also cast as all too human, with flaws and shortcomings, it was Stan Lee, developer of the Marvel Universe, who really brought an overall sense of humanity to the character of the superhero. Many of the Marvel characters had not only the powers that defined their superhero status but also the sorts of struggles that clearly reflected the complexity of human experience. Hulk had an alter ego human character who struggled with managing his emotions. Black Panther's narrative rides on the challenges of becoming a defining figure for his nation in the face of changing world conditions. Jean Grey's story poses questions about how superpowers can impact the success of teams. Through his signature characters, Stan Lee told very human stories, ones that we could better relate to, ones that reflected something of ourselves back to us.

Humanity defines not only our flaws but also our hunger to express ourselves through ingenuity, to problem-solve relationships with our fellow humans, and above all, to love. Often our humanity is mirrored in our interaction with others and thus becomes a powerful theme to living a life beyond satisfying our own needs. As a fundamental character attribute, humanity then becomes a set of behaviors that can motivate our progress from mediocre to extraordinary, and ultimately, to contributing to causes greater than ourselves. Connecting to our humanity offers three distinct benefits.

Realizing your human potential enables you to better realize your superhuman life. The further along we go in life, the more likely we are to recognize how little we can control. One thing we *can* control is our belief in our individual human potential and the potential of humankind. Whenever I limit my mindset and downplay what I could accomplish, I am cultivating a mindset that does not serve the larger goals of a superhuman life. As entrepreneur and philanthropist Kazuo Inamori puts it,

People who accomplish new things in their work are people who believe in their potential. Nothing new or difficult could ever be achieved if you let your current ability determine what you can or cannot do. Human potential expands limitlessly as we continually work to improve. We must always believe in our unlimited potential and maintain an attitude that bravely meets all challenges.

Humanity means that we are subject to universal laws. We have to recognize that there are certain universal laws that we cannot escape in our human experience. Accepting these laws and embracing the lessons that come with these experiences can help us savor every moment of life we have on this earth. Furthermore, such acceptance can challenge us to clarify our objectives and the rationale behind the intentional actions we take every day. It's critical that we recognize these laws—not to be driven by fear, but instead to be driven by, and even inspired by, our human constraints. Think about this: at some point, we will all experience death, whether it is the death of people we know, the death of people we love, or eventually our own death. We will also experience failure. And pain. And joy. And conflict. And conflict resolution. Embracing our humanity as superhumans means that we do not look at these universal human experiences as signals to run, but as signals to engage even more fully with our existence—every single moment we're able to do so. *Carpe diem!*

Everyone dies, but not everyone lives. A limited amount of time is allotted to us, and we use that time well when we live our lives to the fullest. Embracing our humanity means fulfilling the purposes we've determined are ours using the time we have. This is one of the reasons that what we put our creative energy into matters so significantly. We have an opportunity to create a legacy—something that lives on, something that helps others and continues to do so beyond us. Our legacy might have nothing to do with fame, fortune, and power, but everything to do with what we tried to accomplish for ourselves and others during the time we were here. With this focus and drive, even in your darkest moments, you can be vibrant and stay accountable to contributing something truly great to the human experience. I have come to realize that relying on this concept will remind you that even when you are facing hard times, it is worth getting up every day and continuing to design an incredible life.

Integrity

Our integrity—consistent ethical principles and values, often based in some moral or civil structure—is most often tested when we are challenged. Anything that we aspire to do, for ourselves or others, will come with its own set of challenges. And there will be days when we miss the mark and fail. This, too, can be a learning experience. But the stress, the resistance, and the battles—both external and internal—we face to do anything in this life will often come hand in glove with temptations to seek relief from the pressure in less than honorable ways. These are the very moments when we will need our integrity the most. Otherwise, we will suffer the consequences of living a life that is not reliable to others and that lacks truthfulness and accountability to ourselves. Here now are three takeaways as to why integrity is foundational.

You're not in this alone: someone, somewhere, is watching. Accept that someone is watching. Be who you are—unique and brilliant—by design. But understand that the superhuman life will always bring along with it an audience; and to some degree, you will be a role model. In this life, it is difficult to achieve great things without also attracting admirers as well as critics. It comes with the territory. If you are saying one thing and living another, there is someone out there ready to capitalize on that duality. Superhumans are not perfect. On the contrary, they embody every aspect of a life fully lived, which also includes mistakes and failures. But even in those failures and mistakes, find a way to make amends for your errors, to take responsibility for your actions, and to put more energy into aligning with your own integrity. Our twenty-four-hour media world has brought us stories of many superhumans who have faced the realities of bad mistakes and yet later prevailed by growing through their errors.

Integrity is often your only credential. When working with clients through my agency, Forecast Studios, I remember thinking that we had one chance to prove ourselves. In fact, I remember hearing from the CEO of our first client that keeping our commitments was more important than the quality of the work! Our reputation to deliver was at stake, which meant that we tried to dot every *i* and cross every *t*. From the well-documented timesheets to the degree of detail in our proposals, I led our team to be radically transparent and honest about what we were providing to our clients. This taught me an extremely valuable lesson that is paramount for superhumans applying the code in their daily lives: sometimes integrity is your only credential. I can personally tell you that I have won over entire rooms not because of my resume, but because when I walked out of the room, my work *proved* that what was on my resume was indeed true.

Integrity means you are honest about yourself, with yourself. How often do we tell ourselves a story that we feel good about, but that we know is not true? I suffered the consequences of doing this for years until I discovered that integrity mattered just as much with myself as it did with others. In fact, I realized that my integrity started with having self-awareness of my own poor habits and dysfunctional beliefs. I had to recognize my own temptations and acknowledge my own dualities in order to begin to manage them. I also started to understand that there are many people who have achieved great success, wide influence, and deep impact yet still manage to interrogate their character and improve. Superhumans challenge themselves every day to do the same. As our creative core strengthens, we will also grow in confidence to acknowledge the things we can address, the things that are actually out of our control, and how, by design, to construct solutions to go boldly forward.

Humility

We all of us have egos—and this is before and apart from striving to develop our own superpowers. But letting this striving get out of hand to the point of becoming self-centered or overinvested in your own desires and aspirations can short-circuit your creativity and, ultimately, your superhuman goals. In the workplace, I have seen how a lack of humility can come at an extremely high price. In fact, at the first startup I joined, a dearth of humility played a huge role in the battle between the founders and the investors. It became downright ugly and led to the eventual bankruptcy of the company. In the design profession, it is easy to meet super-talented people who have just that—talent—but nothing else in terms of character. Whether they are hearing feedback or giving it, you would think they were the only person in the room. No matter how great you are, humility is a character trait worth nurturing. Humility is beneficial in and of itself, and it also serves us in three principal ways.

Giving praise to others adds value to others. Every day, superhumans are determined to add value to others. They serve others by living for a higher mission or cause. They battle at the front lines and the fringes of humanity, whether in our local schools and hospitals or in communities that are in dire need of creative solutions to big problems. When we praise these people, we are reminding ourselves of their value to society. In the same way, when we praise those around us, we are bringing out the best in them and stoking their creative fire to go boldly forward, while taking the focus off ourselves. When we do the opposite, and spend time either in deflecting blame or in self-admiration, we keep the focus on ourselves. In my work I would sometimes miss this because I thought that my motivations were pure—and that I was seeking not praise but the feedback that I needed to improve. Over time, I have found it much more valuable to give praise, and then when receiving feedback, whether negative or positive, to remember to sincerely say “thank you.” It’s moments like these that keep me open to putting others first, before my own validation.

Superpowers begin with humility. In their book *Ego Free Leadership: Ending the Unconscious Habits that Hijack Your Business*, Brandon Black and Shayne Hughes give a detailed description of ego archetypes, one of them being our "offensive ego." According to Black and Hughes, the offensive ego desires to be respected, acknowledged, and heard. It is insatiable, and you can see it at work in the egotistical person who can't seem to get out of their own way. We have all met these people—we might even at times have been one of them. Before consciously adopting humility as an attribute, I strove to continually prove to others how great I was, and I frequently demanded validation from my peers, professional colleagues, family, and friends. This behavior kept me in an antagonistic cycle that prevented me from being vulnerable and admitting when I did not know something. I could not nurture and develop my innate abilities—or discover new ones—because I had stopped being receptive to any feedback. My ego was in essence putting all my confidence in the critical reviews of others and keeping me from opening my eyes to new possibilities. Truth learned: we should each of us, no matter what we already know, be humble enough to learn more.

Watch out for triggers. It would take an entire book to adequately cover triggers. In fact, a number of leading psychologists have spent decades researching and writing about these emotional stimuli. How do triggers relate to humility? Again, so much about striving to live a superhuman life has to do with how you manage to maintain equilibrium no matter what is happening to you and around you. The more we experience the extremes of success and failure, the more we will have those moments that push us from being humble to ego-indulgent. It is easy to do. I've done it. And I have watched many other really important people around me do it. I have seen CEOs who were humble and open to new ideas and possibilities turning too deeply inward and creating organizational cultures filled with infighting and close-mindedness. I have seen close friends with reliable character fall victim to the all-too-human consequences of the sudden limelight thanks to quick promotions, awards, and successful moments in life. My point is that nobody is immune to falling back into our ego-driven habits, especially as external factors trigger those sorts of thoughts. The trick is to, of course, stay self-aware, but also to continue to create. Using our innate creativity is one of the fastest ways to shut down those loud internal shouts from our ego and refocus our attention on remaining humble, open-minded, and resourceful.

Resilience

Resilience: we love it. Haven't we seen every superhero we've ever admired be knocked down, get back up, and then put themselves together better than ever? In our mythological universe of pop-culture crusaders, we have shown our love of franchises that take the time to tell the story of a character with incredible powers who gets torn apart only to come back stronger and better. Resilience is easy to admire—even easy to write about. It is, unfortunately, extremely difficult to live. Yet resilience is the one attribute that, in the eyes of many who study these things, distinguishes those who accomplish something worthwhile in life from those who do not. It is also the one character attribute that behaves as a muscle: the more external situations work it, the stronger it becomes. Resilience is vital to keeping you moving forward, fueling your progression into future accomplishments. Resilience can be illustrated in any domain—from sports to theater, from politics to the workplace. In all likelihood, depending on the environment you grew up in, or your cultural background and present cultural context, there could be a high degree of resilience already woven into your character. In my profession, more often than not, being the only person in the room who looks like me demands an unshakable core that is not easily thrown by comments or banter that clearly spell bias, unconscious or not. Resilience serves us all in three fundamental ways.

Bouncing back is overvalued; instead, think bouncing forward. I know you've heard it before—how good it is to be able to "bounce back." That is, to recover quickly from a setback, so as to return to whatever your norm was before the event that sent you spiraling in the first place. But here's the reality: you *don't* bounce back. Whatever your normal state or level of success was before, it will look different once you've experienced a metaphorical punch to the gut. The difficult situations, events, and changes that play out in our lives have an impact. They will change our perspective and approach, especially if we are proactive in growing through the pain. Often, I see people searching for what *was*, even though their previous norm is in the past, never to return. I am guilty of the same thing and have managed to waste hours, days, even months trying to figure out how to "come back" from a mistake, a failure, or an injury. That is, until I discovered that there is something better than bouncing back. It's bouncing *forward*, finding the opportunity in the opposition and using that to advance toward your vision in new ways. So, instead of sorting through the rubble, put your energy into what you can control, and focus on what you can do in the future.

Resilience is in the "by design" DNA. When I received my master's degree in Industrial Design from Georgia Tech, I might as well have received a secondary degree in resilience. I can't tell you how many times my design process failed or my work was critiqued so badly I wanted to walk out of the room. Despite my talent and my passion for working as a creative professional, I had woefully underestimated the amount of adaptability and determination I would need to be successful. That is because they don't advertise resilience when they sell you a sleek and beautiful final product. But behind every single object and experience that we love, there is a brutal and visceral story that details the resilience of the people who worked through adversity to bring it to life. Resilience is built into the design process, and any intentional, by-design effort will require you to persist toward your goals even when things aren't working out. Living superhuman-by-design is an identity that requires you to embrace a spirit of stamina and strength, a spirit that looks forward with confidence. More than any other characteristic, I want you to see that resilience empowers us to tap into the best of our creative selves. The most resilient among us recognize our experiences as our life lessons and then design plans to try a new way of achieving a desired outcome.

Resilience is fear's kryptonite. To live superhuman-by-design is to invite failure into your daily life. In other words, as we live in this new way and push our limits through new creative ventures, we will inevitably fail at things. Working to intentionally grow our creative core means that we will sometimes fail in our attempts at implementing new ideas and that we will sometimes also experience rejection and ridicule. Even more, we will have to get up every day attempting to go after our full potential again with the understanding that factors beyond our control will be lurking outside our door. The critiques, the embarrassment, and the rejection that come from attempting to do more and to be more can begin to nurture something negative in our spirit, if we do not guard against it: fear.

Fear is my most controversial friend—always there to keep me humble, but always ready to stunt my growth. Personifying fear is important because it helps us visualize it and subsequently challenge it, in the same way we would challenge a physical obstacle in our path. Superhumans know that resilience is fear's kryptonite. Test it out. If you want to conquer your fears and grow through mistakes, failures, and rejection, act with a resilient attitude toward the bumps you encounter along the road. I have done this in my personal life, especially in the context of relationship failures, and I have lived this through my experiences with many blue-chip companies. In fact, while working at startups in the Valley, I took the same framed motto to every job, always keeping it in view on my desk. In large, bold type, it asked, "What would you do if you weren't afraid?"

As a creative professional often working in uncharted waters within organizational strategies that changed weekly, I needed to build the type of grit-fortified mind to maintain my calm and produce game-changing results in the workplace, all the while keeping my balance at home. I had to carry over my lessons from yesterday to inform what I would do differently tomorrow. This required mental stamina and strength. I had to learn not to dwell on the negative or allow it to derail me. Instead of avoiding the realities of the challenges I faced, I found healthy distractions through going on long walks outside the office. While walking, I listened to uplifting messages from other entrepreneurs or life coaches who talked about pushing through scary, messy moments. Without taking measures to creatively explore how to become more resilient, I would have succumbed to fear and been unable to grow and progress.

Sacrifice

By "sacrifice," I mean giving up something we value for the sake of others. Many of the most successful and influential people aren't just interested in themselves. They are deeply interested in how what they do each day impacts their associates. Now, I want to emphasize that our motivations to positively affect others might be coming from a self-serving place. It's up to you to interrogate the *why* underlying any sacrifice of the things you value most in life in order to help others around you. What is inarguable, though, is that sacrifice is a key attribute of those who live superhuman lives; and by design, it demands that we lose the "me first," egocentric way of thinking in favor of a more worthy approach.

Superhumans make this trade-off every single day. Our glory is fleeting, but the sacrifices we make in order to see a greater mission come to life are memorable. Typically, we associate this quality with the leaders we admire in our lives. When we discuss leaders in history, we often celebrate how they gave up their comforts for the sake of something of greater worth and importance. This is also the quality we associate with a great team member. No matter your personality, this is the one aspect that people will remember the most. As much as I enjoy individual accolades, they are bittersweet goals when they are achieved without the team's reaching new heights. In fact, in my own pursuit of being validated in a design studio, I would often miss the moment to put the team first. In the end, I found myself rendered as a talented but self-interested designer without the commitment to a greater cause. You won't be able to take flight into a superhuman life if you devalue sacrificing for others and for a cause more worthy than yourself.

To make a sacrifice that matters, we must consider three key principles that are often illustrated viscerally, whether in fiction or reality.

Sacrifice, by design, is not an afterthought. When I design a product or an experience, each design I make is not an afterthought. In fact, the very beginning of the design process is about gaining understanding. When I am in the Empathizing phase, I am learning about both the explicit and the latent needs of the audience I am serving. I am also trying to bring my best to the team, sometimes covering our gaps in the process. The very exercise of this phase of the design process is about forethought. Often the entire design team enters into the design process ready to make sacrifices for the good of the project. While designing in startup environments, I found that some of my best creative partners were willing to give up comfortable, well-paying opportunities so they could be in the trenches of a more challenging environment. Instead of a big salary, they were often motivated by the mission of the project and the camaraderie and selflessness of the design team.

In the same way, adopting a sacrificial, "others-first" mindset in our daily interactions with the world must be intentional and it must be practiced. Our natural tendency is to avoid discomfort and to spend time elevating our own wants and aspirations above those of the group. More often than not, investing energy in the people around us is an afterthought, something we do only after our own self-serving goals have been met. I encourage you to adopt the sacrificial mindset early in all of your engagements. We can creatively ideate and design ways to communicate to others that we are fully present for them and their success. Mentors and coaches do this all the time in an effort to build rapport with their mentees or teams. By doing so, you'll become a superhuman who produces dynamic and extraordinary results not just for yourself but for others as well.

The endurance factor. Do you remember the show *Fear Factor*? It was a game show back in the early 2000s (I know, seems like forever ago) that challenged contestants to face their wildest fears for the reward of a cash prize. Host Joe Rogan and anxious audiences would watch contestants compete against each other in a variety of extreme stunts that would test them physically and mentally. Often the winner was not the most courageous or even the bravest contestant. The winner was rather the person who endured the longest. That person was the last contestant, the one to walk away with the prize money in their pocket. These contestants committed to sacrificing their comforts and allaying their worries long enough to win. They had the stamina and the willpower to go beyond their fear-plagued thoughts and act with bravery. In much the same way, as we learn to endure difficult situations, we gain the ability to manage the constant desire to satisfy our every want and need. Ultimately, the endurance factor can help us dial down the impulse to make the world all about us, so that we act instead in service of others and the greater needs of our communities.

Making sacrifices is a means to an end. When we look at a typical superhero arc, there is usually a moment when they are putting themselves in harm's way for the benefit of others. Superheroes give us a chance to imagine the feeling of giving up something valuable—in many cases our very lives—for others. We watch these narratives, hoping for the best outcome, because the superheroes will be protected by their superpowers and their near-perfect invulnerability. As we watch people in real life whom we think of as superheroes, we understand that their attempt to do something more in a critical moment is characterized by the sacrifices they make. Every day, public servants act in heroic ways to save the lives of others. Imagine a world with no honest police officers to keep the peace, no nurses to save lives, no firefighters to rescue residents in burning buildings—that would mean more daily chaos for all of us. We inherently know that the women and men who dedicate their lives to these lines of work are making huge sacrifices.

In this way, making a sacrifice is a means to an end. Superhumans recognize that they are leaders, and as leaders in a position of visibility, they must sometimes make sacrifices to see a shared mission through to the end. Superhumans model a sacrificial attitude by weighing the reasons they are willing to forgo their own benefit for the sake of something greater. I love author and motivational speaker Simon Sinek's movement to dig deeper into the reasons you do what you do, encapsulated in his challenge to audiences to "Find Your WHY." His work speaks to passion and inspiration, to making space for others to be great, to building a better world together. As we look more deeply into the components of a superhuman life, you will see that by designing a vision with others in mind, the sacrifices you make will have purpose, significance, and tremendous worth for others.

CHALLENGES TO LIVING SUPERHUMAN BY DESIGN

If creativity is the fuel for a superhuman life, the Superhuman Code is its moral compass. The code is a set of principles to help guide the decisions we make as we travel our life's path. Each of us must explore what these attributes mean for us personally, and how we will apply them. Taking a look at the code also enables us to examine this path objectively to see whether it's for us.

One of the biggest challenges to staying on this path, if we have chosen it, is continuing to be guided by the code even in the face of failure—or sometimes success! This is the challenge of maintaining our character no matter what. Our natural tendency as humans is to deviate from our principles and values when facing great success or great failure. Our deepest character attributes are often tested in these moments, and we have to determine whether to operate from a place of shifting feelings and emotions or from a strong character base.

Sun Tzu, an ancient Chinese military strategist and general, said that a moral compass brings people into accord with their ruler, so that they will follow him in life and in death without fear. He recorded his thoughts in *The Art of War*, highly regarded even today by leaders not only in the military but also in the corporate world. Many of its principles have practical application, while others provide a grounding in philosophical considerations.

Though a moral compass does not necessarily provide the *motivation* for maintaining a resolute attitude in moments of astounding success or astounding failure—and while, outside of war, we're not looking for a battle to the death—a solid moral compass does provide the grounding in character that guards against the circumstances of our lives taking control of our will and reshaping it.

The path to altering our lives for the better is often messy. It will be filled with moments of success and moments where we miss the mark. In order to reach our maximum potential, we must minimize our vulnerability to being controlled and guided by temporary, external circumstances, whether positive or negative. If superhumans lose their sense of an ethical code, they in essence lose the internal compass required to keep them focused on delivering extraordinary results for themselves and those in their lives. It is this steadfastness of character, despite circumstances, that lifts them above average.

No doubt you have already experienced this, but anything of significance we hope to achieve will inevitably be difficult. There will be disappointments when we do not reach the goals we are striving for or when we suffer setbacks along the way. But we will also be vulnerable to the pleasures of success, which will tempt us to open ourselves to distractions, comforts, and departure from the qualities that brought us these momentary wins in the first place. Both extremes can take us away from our best creative selves, inviting us to focus on our egos, threatening to dismantle the daily practices that have grounded us. Superhumans, by their very nature, embrace the realities of the world and then do everything possible to make the most of it and even change it for the better, for all concerned.

In summary, the superhuman-by-design life is not about, on the one hand, being content with one-time success or, on the other, being completely defeated by one-time failures or disappointments. The superhuman-by-design life is also not without its challenges.

In fact, as you'll see in Part Two, often we ourselves construct the barriers that block us from effectively exploring new avenues in our journey to maximizing our potential. By applying the code alongside the design process that operationalizes our creativity, we are ultimately on the path to living extraordinary lives, filled with fulfillment, significance, and life-altering changes.

In Parts 2 and 3, I will walk you through tangible examples that will help you develop and unleash your creative self so as to live superhuman-by-design. In the end, my hope is that you will join me on the path of constantly looking into your life with the intention and purpose of producing impactful, life-changing, superhuman results.

IN THE VALLEY

INTERLUDE

In the late summer of 2013, I knew that my life was about to take a huge change in course. My time at IDEO had been an intense roller coaster of feelings and emotions. The Boston culture had been difficult to adjust to, in part, because of the hyper-localization of the neighborhoods. Though I was trying to adjust to the local culture, it felt like my relationships with others were primarily superficial. And my first winter there seemed to last forever. In short, I was exhausted and wanted to figure out a new path.

So, when I was approached by a previous creative director for a new opportunity in San Francisco, I knew it was time to make a shift. I just did not know how much of a shift I was about to make.

Transitioning to the Bay Area was one of the most consequential decisions of my life. Not only did it change the outlook on my career, it expanded my perspective on and understanding of business. I had always felt like an entrepreneur, but I had never been in an environment that encouraged me to mix my creativity with my desire to birth new products and platforms into the world. For me, coming to the Bay Area meant getting an invitation to the epicenter of the creative world: Silicon Valley.

One of my most vivid memories is sitting on the top floor of the grand and historic Mark Hopkins Hotel at Mason and California Streets, atop Nob Hill, and looking out over the city while having breakfast. It was at that very moment I knew my entire life would change forever.

During this time, the Valley, and specifically San Francisco, was experiencing one of the greatest growth spurts of anywhere in the US. People were flocking in from all areas of the world to pursue new jobs, new companies, and new ideals. There was a wealth of opportunity available, and I knew that I wanted to be a part of it. Everywhere I looked, dilapidated buildings were being quickly converted into shiny new offices for tech-oriented transplants. Companies we are all now familiar with were teeming with magnetic energy, just getting started in a new era for the Bay. Their names became even bigger as more investment money flooded the Valley in those years—names like Uber, Airbnb, and Slack.

Meanwhile, the giants of the Valley were looming larger than ever, recruiting some of the brightest and most creative minds from the top colleges in the country. These companies are now global household names everywhere—companies like Google, Netflix, Amazon, Apple, and Facebook.

It was an exciting time to be the Bay Area and to live in San Francisco. Even more, I had come to the Valley to work as a designer, with the goal of becoming a creative leader in an organization. At this time, *design* was the hottest word on the block. Anyone who was a designer was regarded as a creative and visionary gem. Almost every company seemed to be hiring talented designers and engineers. Though I had transitioned to San Francisco with a big company, my hope was to soon become a part of a fledging startup that would rise to the top of the heap and give me the epic ride of a lifetime to success and financial freedom.

Everywhere I turned, I saw twenty-something people, wrapped in urban-chic looks, running about the city. They were from all over the country, even the world, and they all seemed to be in the city for the same things. Though I had joined a company that had been around for over fifty years, I soon found myself swept up in a modern-day gold rush: it was the wave of startup culture, and by the time I entered my second year in the Bay, a tsunami of new ideas and companies was overtaking the city.

Weekly, I heard about yet another company raising Series A financing. For those unfamiliar with startup financing, Series A financing refers to an investment in a privately held, often fledgling, startup company. The company usually has to show its potential to grow, to generate revenue, and to capture the hearts and minds of a big audience ready to hit "subscribe" or check out from its online stores. Even more exciting for me was to track a startup with a great concept as it went from raising money through crowdsourcing, meaning tapping into investment from a loyal group of followers, to being funded by a group of major investors.

And the numbers weren't small.

Sometimes it was a few million. But by early 2015, it was not unusual to hear about companies raising tens of millions of dollars in Series A funding and then going on to raise even more millions in subsequent rounds of funding. It was a coming-of-age moment for many people in the city because so many of us were transplants from elsewhere, meaning that we'd never before experienced the pace of urban change that we were experiencing now in San Francisco. The days often moved from long hours in the office to evenings full of networking and events. Many of us had to learn how to navigate the responsibility of taking care of ourselves, all while surviving the booming dynamics of this thriving city, our new home.

For me, it was difficult to resist the temptation to ride the wave to wealth and the clout that would come from being part of a Cinderella startup story. The titles given out to new employees were just as mouth-watering as the six-figure salaries, bonuses, and equity packages given in informal job offers. But it wasn't just the money or the title, it was the lifestyle the visionaries painted: "We can be the next Apple," "We can do the impossible," "We can revolutionize the world!" It was a self-aggrandizing era, where more often than not the CEOs of the startups were guys (and precious few gals) in their late twenties and early thirties. Each person I met in that position seemed to have a bigger ego than the last. And the more successful their product, the more they would promote their story to any audience.

In the spring of 2015, an opportunity in the startup universe landed on my plate. It was hard to resist. You see, in just two short years, I'd experienced some of my highest highs and some of my lowest lows. I had led the global launch of the lauded Dolby Cinema while working as a creative director in the Dolby marketing organization. The launch made millions for the company and revolutionized the modern cinema experience for its consumer audience. We won several design awards and nabbed the attention of a few celebrated media partners. I was traveling to all the famous movie studios—Universal, MGM, Warner Brothers, and even Pixar.

But, privately, I was living through a difficult personal separation and the subsequent relationship fallout with old friends and colleagues in my network. The roller coaster of ups and downs led me to spend more time with visionaries chasing audacious goals. These were the people I considered to be the "shapers"—exuberantly building the future and bringing along talented, creative people who thirsted for more. At the time, I saw the startup life as a way to supercharge my climb to the top.

Eventually, I transitioned from Dolby and joined a company that at the time was called Skully Helmets. It soon changed its name to Skully. It was in this transition that I found myself in a vein that pulsed me straight to the artery of the action I wanted so badly. I was in the heart of the Valley, striving to eclipse my recent smaller successes and failures in one huge exit.

What followed eighteen months later was one of the most spectacular and epic ends to any of the startups in recent Valley history. It deserves an HBO documentary special. When the doors to the company closed, it was the end of an arduous startup experience—but certainly not the end of my startup journey. Only through this journey did I make many of the discoveries I am sharing with you in this book. I came to those revelations through the lenses of designer and entrepreneur, and it is through these lenses that I hope to illustrate for you the methods and principles that became deeply instrumental in my personal and professional growth over these tumultuous years. This is how *Superhuman-by-Design* was born.

The point of sharing some of these startup stories is to help you see how seductive the allure of achieving impossible results can be. Even for those of us who might not revel in the desire to be a part of something great, it is extremely hard to resist the potential of having more, so much more, than we have now. Such desire drives the human spirit, and this is why even the greatest athletes, performers, and leaders seem to want more and more, despite having already attained so much.

The startup culture plucked these strings perfectly, and with so many conversations about success and money happening around me, I found myself fighting to maintain my values and ethics. The materialism was only one aspect that kept me burning the midnight oil many a night for a startup CEO. It was also the deep, unquenchable desire to be recognized as having done something greater, something bigger than life.

But at this stage, I did not yet have the self-awareness to understand why I wanted a "superhuman result," a result that seemed greater than my imagination. I could picture what the experience would be like for any creative leader who found himself or herself at the top of the startup conversation. I dreamed of the influence and the platform that I would have, and I also marveled at the thought of not laboring up the ladder in a big, dusty company, but rather riding the elevator smoothly and swiftly to the shiny new top. The moral quandaries of this time in my life taught me that achieving success purely for success's sake is one of the most unfulfilling experiences that anyone, even a driven person, can live through.

Even more, as a Black man in the city during this era, I found myself striving to prove my intelligence and capability to a primarily white, tech-focused audience and to showcase my success to a Black audience, hoping to receive those accolades due anyone from the community who achieved something considered applause-worthy.

It was not until my first startup, Skully, went bankrupt in the late summer of 2016 that I began to understand not only that my disruptive path toward the summit was no longer serving me well, but also that it was not serving, and had never served, a greater good. At that time, the momentum of running with the startup culture was too strong to pivot from, but my personal mission of creating extraordinary, life-changing results was, shall we say, challenged.

Being a part of a bankruptcy can do that to you.

It is deeply emotional to lose your job.

And it is absolutely crushing to watch your friends—not just colleagues, but *friends*, people you have sweated with and cried with through the struggle of bringing something to the world—slowly pack their desks and fill boxes with their belongings and head out the door. It was an absolutely defeating time, one that I will never forget. The more so because our team had created so much monetary success and we had drawn to ourselves such a significant online following.

I had earned thousands of dollars, more than I had ever had in my entire life, but it did not matter because as the creative director of the team, I had to watch as our online channels burned with fire from angry customers and investors. I scrolled through tons of online headlines that read like a Netflix special. The startup blogs wrote about the soap opera sweetheart company that had rocketed to a stratosphere other startups could only dream about, only to tumble, crash, and burn. It was embarrassing, painful, and humbling. It marked a failure in our leadership, and ultimately, a moment in which I did not know where to turn next.

This is when *Superhuman by Design* flared into life. It came out of the fight to stay above water that was my life post-Skully. It brought me back to a place where I started to question why I was doing what I was doing. To what end? Whom was I serving? Why did I spend my days going after these superficial achievements and craving material results?

For the first time in years, I questioned why I was pushing what I was pushing forward into the world. I still knew that I did not want to be mediocre or just average, but I was also ready for a new adventure: exploring how to build a fulfilling, gratifying life that sought superhuman results for something much more significant than merely a superficial kind of success.

Throughout this book, my goal is to inspire you with my anecdotes and superhero references, and to help you visualize where I am coming from and why the superhuman-by-design life is a life worth pursuing. I want you to be able to apply the lessons from my experiences in service of achieving your own goals, both privately and professionally. Though I hope that you find these details useful and instructive, my primary goal is for you to unlock your own creative core so that you can be your boldest and most successful self—your superhuman self.

POWER

PART TWO

POWERS, PILLARS, AND RESULTS

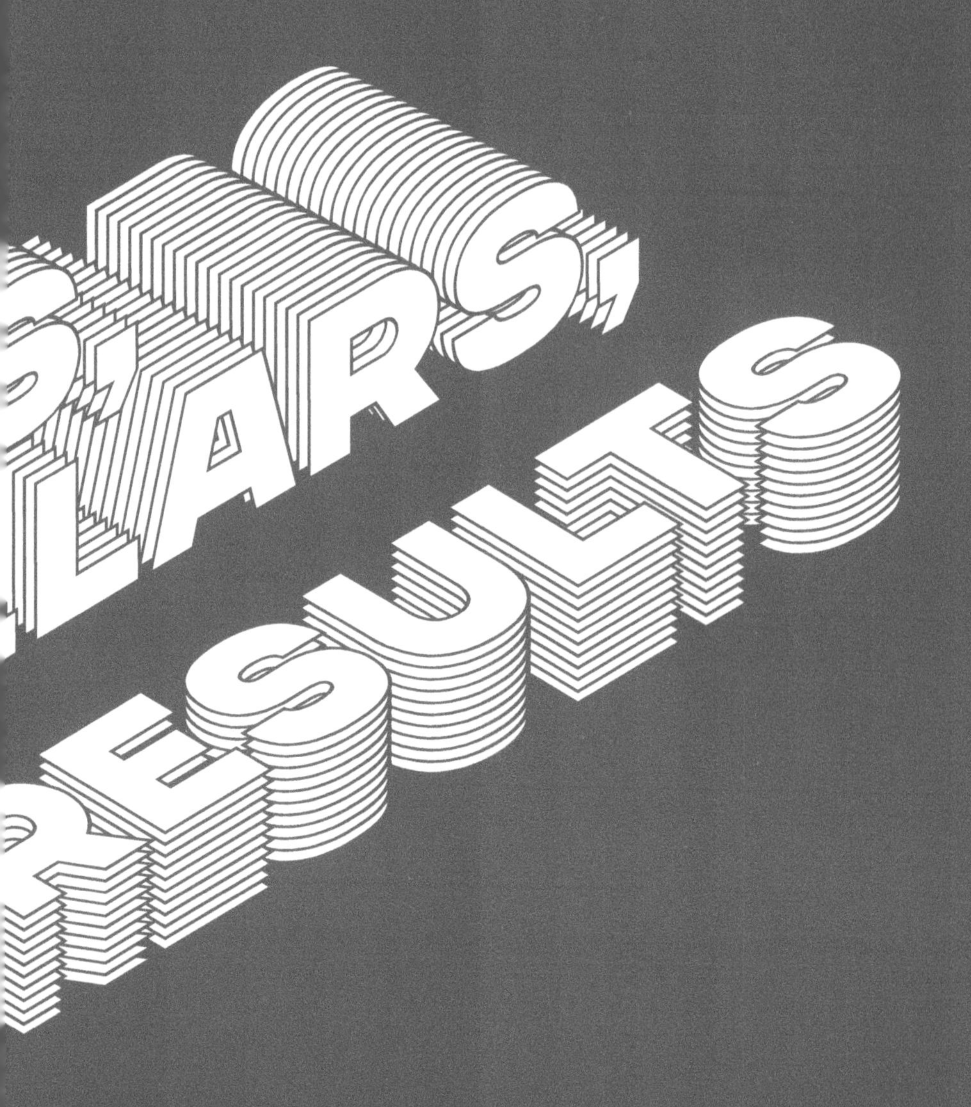

THE FOUNDATIONAL SUPERPOWERS

As superhumans, we are to live a life of impact, influence, and significance beyond ourselves and our own needs. People are the greatest daily reminder of why we are to be superhuman as often as possible. Our loved ones, our colleagues, our classmates, and the other people we interact with each day all play a part in how we experience the world—just as we, in turn, play a part in how *they* experience the world.

Each of us has innate talents and abilities. These are our *superpowers*. The more we use these powers for good—the more we are able to help those around us in a life-giving way—the more of a boost we'll give others in living better, more productive, more satisfying lives. As we leverage our superpowers to promote positive attitudes and outcomes for the people around us, we promote a greater good in our communities, our families, and society overall.

But often, we do not understand what those powers are and how we can access them on command. Understanding how to access our superpowers is absolutely critical to living superhuman-by-design.

And how do we do that? By developing our creative core and living with intention and purpose. Think of the superpowers listed here as the starter set. They are foundational. As you work intentionally in your own life, you will build on these foundational powers, augmenting and tailoring them for yourself, and you will discover others of your own.

THE SUPERPOWERS

I've illustrated these superpowers with examples from my own life, to show how I've used them and to suggest ways in which you might work with them as well. In the next chapter, I'll offer some simple exercises you can use to identify and codify more superpowers you might have, based on your talents, whether innate or developed.

Breathing

Discovering the power of breathing was one of the most revolutionary moments of my life. Every breath we take is critical to our ability to function as healthy human beings. We hear about the benefits of mindful breathing all the time. In sports and in meditation. In yoga and in the hospital. The power of the human breath is tied to our very existence. In fact, one of our most celebrated holy texts begins with God himself breathing life into man. In the book of Genesis, chapter 2, verse 7, we read:

> ***Then the Lord God formed man of dust from the ground, and breathed into his nostrils the breath of life; and man became a living being.***

Now, you might be wondering, why is taking a moment to breathe a superhuman ability? It is because the majority of people do not do this. Instead, all too often, breathing is an automatic action that requires very little thought, if any. To undertake it more thoughtfully, we have to turn our attention to the act of breathing.

Why is this important? Think about a moment in which you've experienced resistance on your journey to accomplishing a goal. Perhaps you've felt it when taking an exam, when preparing for a speech or presentation, or in a moment of conflict with a colleague, manager, or family member. Each day we all experience levels of resistance that build up a tremendous amount of toxins in our bodies and anxiety in our minds. To maintain a sense of composure and control, we can learn how to control our breathing. Commanding our breath can be the deciding factor in how we react to any situation or circumstance.

This is a superhuman ability that has incredible benefits in every area of our lives, including our faith, our finances, and most importantly, our relationships with our fellow human beings. So, let's explore how to master our breathing.

As a designer and eventually a director at some of the most lauded design agencies in the industry, I have personally suffered from the lack of aptitude or maturity to manage my emotional skills. Becoming a brilliant and effective communicator can be achieved, but it requires daily dedication to focusing on your breathing. Though dismissed by many as a simple exercise, breathing with focus and control can open our brains to new levels of creativity and innovation.

While working on a big project for a Japanese global supplier at IDEO, I experienced a very frustrating moment with the project leader of our team. While going back and forth over a design decision requiring some technical understanding, we found ourselves arguing loudly within the project space. In that moment, the leader told me his answer was correct because he had attended Stanford and I had attended an industrial design program at Georgia Tech that was not of the same caliber.

Now, I understand that this was his way of trying to quickly end the discussion and discourage me from contending any further. It was also his way of establishing a dominant role in front of the rest of the team.

But at that moment in my career, I did not have the maturity to handle the interaction. Instead of pausing and moving into a moment of breathing to regain my composure, I responded with some angry comments that did not reflect my character or serve our relationship well through the remainder of the project.

This experience rattled me because I knew my character was one that was inclusive and peaceable. I wanted to be collaborative, and typically I have a very patient and accommodating attitude with my managing directors. But, as I came to learn, all of us suffer from the impulse to react when faced with resistance or conflict.

We also sometimes go into a panic when we experience a challenging circumstance or individual. Instead, imagine mastering the ability to breathe so thoroughly that you can lower your heart rate at will and fully guide your thoughts and desires. Imagine in a moment of passion, conflict, or friction being able to fully control your breathing and command yourself successfully.

If you miss the opportunity to train yourself in the ability of being mindful about your breath, you will not be prepared for those moments when you must control your breathing the most. To gain control of your breath, it is absolutely critical to practice it every day through meditation and mindfulness, even while taking breaks at work. Keep in mind, too, that our existence does not depend on the breath we just took; it depends on the one we will take next. Just as we cannot achieve levels of success and significance by being backward thinkers instead of forward thinkers, we cannot rely on our last breath. It is already behind us.

Your breathing is your life.

Your breathing is your first source of creative fuel to access your other superhuman abilities. If breathing is underestimated, you will lack the power to access the other superhuman abilities at your disposal. I have become a big advocate of controlling my breathing because it supports my ability to be creative. Breathing leads to consciousness, an acute, present awareness of our senses. And it enables us to refine our sense of awareness about how other people in the room are feeling.

As we breathe, especially in social settings, we become that much more engaged with and attuned to the conversations happening around us and with us. Deliberate, conscious breathing gives us an enhanced ability to listen and to interpret the words and intent of others. As we breathe, our conscious selves are prepared to face friction with confidence and creativity, and to address the challenges ahead with our teams, our colleagues, and our communities.

Magnetism

Superhumans know that people can be won over. The power of winning people over to your point of view, especially in the context of the marketplace, involves making micro-investments into them through what you share and how you connect those shared goals and experiences back to the project.

As a creative leader, it is absolutely critical to understand that by adding value to your team, you are ultimately building equity toward superhuman outcomes.

Perhaps we have learned the value of encouraging others, passing the credit to others, and trying to serve others before serving ourselves. But the power to win people over comes through reminding them why their effort is so critical to the success of the project. By emphasizing the significance of their contribution, you are investing in helping them win. And everyone wants to win.

I had a prime reminder of this when launching Dolby Cinema, an incredible feat and to this day one of the most challenging experiences of my entire career. It required building relationships with people globally, and the work was both asynchronous and synchronous over the course of many months. At one point, I was responsible for three theater sites under construction in the US and abroad. I had teams in Barcelona, Spain; Los Angeles; and the Netherlands. I had to figure out how to build fluid communication between a number of groups in order to successfully launch the new cinemas. In other words, I needed to behave in a superhuman way and generate some extraordinary results.

To achieve successful launches of the theaters, I employed my superpower of winning people over. It started with communicating the vision of the Dolby Cinema to everyone involved at every theater site—and I mean *everyone*, down to the employees working the concession stands. I knew that if it was to work, my dream of opening the world's greatest cinema experience had to become *their* dream. I knew they had to buy into delivering an experience with a great reputation. I put as much energy as possible into reminding people how special it was to be associated with the project, pointing out why, too, their contribution was so significant.

By the time we were close to launching, even the janitors at every site were going through the theaters three or four times a day to make sure that everything looked spectacular. Everyone involved at every site began to see me as the champion of the Dolby Cinema concept and to attribute the success of the launches to my efforts to build congruence and synergy with everyone involved. And it was bringing everyone along in the vision that made us successful. We did it together.

The superpower of magnetism has since played a significant role in developing my creative core and in helping me achieve life-changing results in many areas of my life. Even more, magnetism is a compounding superpower, meaning that the more successful you are at winning people over, the more they will share your aspirations and hopes with others.

As a volunteer in my local community, I am amazed at organizers who can rally large groups of people for everything from voting campaigns to citywide protests. Over the years, I have adopted their willingness to constantly figure out ways to inspire and motivate people around shared missions or values. These superhumans are always helping others by pointing people to resources to help them grow and achieve community-level goals. In time, they become magnets in a growing network of influential and exceptional individuals seeking out higher-value causes.

In my personal experience, I find that by sharing my journey boldly through professional forums, local design panels, and even lifestyle podcasts, I inspire more people to value creativity as well as the design process. My effort to share with all types of audiences allows me to reach people with titles above mine who often have wider connections and more community influence. The superpower of magnetism has also allowed me to build a community of followers who represent those coming behind me—college students and high schoolers all over the country.

So, if you want game-changing results and extraordinary outcomes in your life, begin winning people over, both in your immediate world and beyond your network, through magnetism. You can leverage this power to go beyond your insecurities and focus on saying what needs to be said to unlock the potential of people and help them see the unique part their story plays in the compelling story of a project, a company, or your community.

Rebooting

We often associate intelligence with the ability to think of solutions, especially under pressure. We think of people who are solution-oriented as intelligent problem-solvers. We might compare ourselves to people like that and think, "If only I were smarter," or "If only I could figure that out." Well, there is a superpower that we can access daily to help us reframe challenges and see them from a new perspective. It is the ability to reset the mind.

Our culture is familiar now with the concept of "resetting." Years of cable boxes and video game consoles have given way to other personal consumer electronics, phones, and laptops. As a designer, I have had to hit the physical buttons on devices many times to instruct a product to run a startup script. We can generally see the benefits of such resetting immediately. The device is now ready for new software. Odd device errors often disappear.

But what about people resetting their minds? I am not necessarily referring to recovering from a traumatic, life-altering experience, though we do see superhumans bouncing forward from some of the most desperate tragedies. Rather, I'm talking about the speed bumps we all experience. The days we face creative roadblocks. The days we can't seem to focus on what we need to accomplish and so fail to deliver on our promises and commitments. Or even the days we experience a failure and must continue forward with our remaining responsibilities.

What if we could access the ability to reset our minds? To "reset" in a few minutes from any discouragement and then surge forward with positive momentum? How would we grow such a power? How could we access it to quickly enter a superhuman, transcendent mindset, enabling us to deliver excellent results no matter the circumstances?

Have you ever watched an athlete in a game or competition make a strong comeback after a momentary setback? All of us have seen a moment in which an athlete does something that seems superhuman, leading to seemingly supernatural results. One minute, they can seem absolutely defeated, and the next, they've found that second wind that changes the outcome of a game or an event.

The first way to access the superpower of resetting the mind is to keep reminders of your greater purpose visible and near you throughout the day. Athletes are great at doing this. Sometimes you'll see a pitcher in Major League Baseball use a focus trigger to reset after giving up a home run to an opposing team. Focus triggers are signals, albeit simple ones, that when employed can tell the brain and body to refocus and lock in on the task at hand. One way I achieve this is to identify something tangible that triggers my mind to stop dwelling on what went wrong or is going wrong, and to put my attention instead on the task at hand. Think about what specific artifacts and objects you can create in your own space—these are the visual anchors that will serve as your focus triggers. Decide what visual anchors you can reference and whether what you have around you is helping you reset your mind when the circumstances don't look to be in your favor.

Sometimes the goals we pursue aren't focused on an immediate task, but rather are long-term and intangible—for example, a promotion, a degree, or a certificate. On occasion, the goal might take the form of something less visible, like mental or spiritual growth. As we march toward those goals, we will make mistakes and, occasionally, we will be very wrong. As we recognize these moments during the day, the week, or even the month, we can take advantage of the power to reset our minds by making our big-picture goals visible and tangible. We can generate these reminders in all types of ways—everything from motivational posters or brochures to Pinterest boards full of inspiring images.

So, as opposed to mindlessly scrolling through social media, seeking inspiration and relief in an endless news feed, turn your attention to the things that help your mind focus on the "now" and an optimistic future. Superhumans don't reboot their minds through escaping into distraction—in fact, distractions will do the opposite of resetting your mind by investing your energy in wasteful emotions. Distractions can tend to discourage us, leaving us full of anxiety or feeling down about our mistakes. Keeping our big-picture purpose front and center can remind us of why we are doing what we do.

As I prepared *Superhuman-by-Design* over the course of two years, there were so many times that I blundered in my discipline to write. Some days I had writer's block, and other days I just lost the belief that the book could be meaningful to others. As I labored to bring this book to life, I surrounded myself with books from self-published authors. In time, my desk was a trophy case of well-read books, primarily from first-time authors who had managed to endure the test of delivering a book to the world. Whenever I was discouraged, I would glance over at the stacks and manage to eke out another paragraph.

Teleportation

Color is absolutely critical to the success of any branding campaign. Designers, creatives, and those who work in the fashion and advertising industry base million-dollar decisions on color. A color's hue and vibrancy can alter the way we perceive a product or an environment.

If you have ever debated which color to paint the walls in a particular room, you know how important it is to make sure the color is rich and vibrant, and to get it just right. For a second, close your eyes and imagine what this experience must be like for artists who work at companies like Pixar and Disney. When these artists create new feature films or theme park rides, they are dreaming up novel, vibrant experiences meant to transport us to new worlds. They are constantly seeking to "wow" through narratives that are bright and daring and that leave us with a sense of wonder and awe.

The superhuman ability to access worlds that we envision is the principal power that has driven so many successful companies in Silicon Valley. It is the disruptive force that pushes what seems impossible in terms of technology and leads to the seamless experiences and consumer products we love. The bold vision of these companies becomes a self-fulfilling prophecy. As the CEOs of these companies believe, so they achieve. The once seemingly "impossible" things we do now with technology were first envisioned by designers and engineers and forward thinkers who could imagine a future world and then design toward that end.

Many of us dream of lives bursting at the seams with love, laughter, success, and accomplishment. We seek to live a vibrant existence, to be as brilliant as possible with our family, in our relationships with friends, and even with our colleagues. We imagine fulfilling travel goals, living healthy lives, and even having substantial rewards for our efforts in our community or networks. But sometimes we feel a certain "dullness" come upon us from our brush with everyday struggles or unexpected obstacles. When we do experience a "parting of the clouds," that momentary flash can often fade as rapidly as it appeared. Then, it is back to the average, daily grind of responsibility and stress.

But what if we could part the clouds more often? What if we could even part them on demand? Imagine being able to find new solutions to challenges or coming up with creative plans to bring new ideas to life.

What if you had the power to open portals—mental windows to imagine and explore new vistas—to anywhere, from anywhere?

We have seen people do this in every imaginable place in life. In fact, this is why the stories of those facing steep odds resonate so deeply with us. Documentary-style biopics and Hollywood movies like *Slumdog Millionaire* and *The Pursuit of Happyness* show our general interest in people who seem to be able to imagine a bigger, bolder future. And though the protagonist often seems the least likely to succeed, these underdogs end up having tremendous success, often eclipsing the world where they started. They have seen beyond the limitations of now. They have seen through a portal to alternate solutions or plans.

When we open that invisible gateway to a greater us, we see a more brilliant, vibrant person operating at maximum capacity. And this is an "us" that leaves an inspiring and uplifting impression on everyone we interact with during that time. Think about those people who come into our lives for only a moment, but who leave a tremendous impression by "pulling back the curtain" on our potential. A few minutes with someone like this can help us imagine and discover a more fulfilled version of ourselves. Just as we can do with others.

You can access this power so as to be vibrant and to radiate vibrancy, on command.

We do this by first setting aside time to turn off the constant noise and distraction for moments of meditation and mindfulness. With these moments, we can transform our attitudes from "follower attitudes," often full of doubt, insecurity, and lack of knowledge, to "leader attitudes," filled with confidence, security, and information. With these moments we will, in time, begin thinking completely differently from the common approaches. By recording these moments in our journals and calendars, we can begin building a system of thinking that produces game-changing, and often life-changing, results. If you struggle to write, there are many techniques, such as recording self-talk and affirmations to capture your goals, vision, and ideas. In my own practice, I leverage playlists of rainforest sounds or apps with calming soundscapes to imagine myself solving a present challenge, but in a different location.

As you practice the power of teleportation, goals that before seemed too big to accomplish now become targets that are too big to miss. And realities that you thought were too far away will now be closer than ever.

Accessing these portals for ourselves enables us to develop an attitude that others around us will perceive as superhuman. If you too practice opening such portals, you will soon be regarded as the boldest person in the room with the most out-of-the-box solutions. You will have fresh perspectives to offer and novel solutions to introduce time and time again. Even more, discovering the superhuman ability to access portals through what you envision can not only take you to another level but also help you to help others succeed.

Shapeshifting

One of the most feared foes of Marvel's X-Men superhero franchise is a mutant named Mystique. Her power to mimic the appearance and voice of any person with an almost indiscernible precision makes her incredibly dangerous. Her ability to take on the powers of others is even more intimidating. The more exposure she has to other characters, the more her abilities expand.

Imagine having the uncanny ability to mimic the capabilities and powers of others around you! Imagine not knowing the limit of this power—that is, imagine a power that is plastic, limited only by the degree of exposure to situations that would demand its value.

The superhuman who maximizes their ability to shapeshift will experience the incredible, undeniable, and exponential growth that arrives through perpetual flexibility and adaptability. This means that the more we can learn how to grow through any circumstance or situation by allowing ourselves to absorb lessons from the most successful people, behaviors, and elements of that environment, the more we will be able to drive impact and successful outcomes. This does not mean that we deny our true identities, but rather that we embrace the superhuman condition of being able to shift ourselves to the most valuable elements of our environments.

We often see this level of shapeshifting in financially successful communities of immigrant families. While we could identify levels of assimilation in their behaviors and attitudes, they are still often characterized as maintaining their culture and belief systems. How is it, then, that they are able to thrive in a new environment? They have leaned into the superhuman ability to shapeshift.

For a period of time, they adopt the most successful habits of their environment so that they're able to maximize their potential outcomes. They take advantage of immediate elements and benefits around them to be successful. They also study the habits of predecessors who have succeeded or even thrived in the environment and implement these learnings into their daily practice. They quickly take huge, actionable steps to mimic the success factors immediately around them and implement these practices consistently in hopes of improving their lives and increasing their personal income.

It is this power that a company taps into when hiring talented creative leaders as opposed to only "creative talent." A successful creative leader can mimic the best, most aspirational characteristics of a brand—literally embodying the brand in their daily lives. As a result, they will have a direct influence on the social experience and the attitudes of the creatives around them.

While at Coca-Cola, I experienced the superhuman ability to shapeshift for the first time and immediately saw how it could bring new levels of success into my life. The vice president of the creative department won over the demanding marketing leadership by often mirroring their lightheartedness or playful anxiousness during creative reviews. His ability to transform his mannerisms for the duration of the meeting to mirror their quips and energy made him a star with the marketing team. They would often wear Coca-Cola colors in their outfits: red, black, silver, and white. So, on the days we had creative walkthroughs with the marketing team, he would have all of the creatives wear these colors to show our pride in the Coca-Cola brand.

We Americans saw something similar with our forty-fourth president, Barack Obama. He showed the American people and the world his ability to attune himself to the audience he was addressing or the people he was interacting with. His uncanny ability to meet those in the room around him on their own ground in an authentic way made him a well-respected and well-loved figure around the world. He was able to try foods, dances, and languages in countries where other presidents had not made inroads. He often reflected the energy of his competition in Congress back to its members. If they took a more dramatic tone, he would patiently wait, interpret, and then deliver a response that mirrored their energy, but with more skill and articulation. While many historians may question the administrative effectiveness of Obama, his ability to inspire people by embracing the most celebrated aspects of their values and local culture will forever confirm him as one of the most successful communicators and connectors in modern history.

When you dive into the superhuman ability to relate to people, you will begin to experience the tremendous benefits that come with it. You will discover another level of humanity that helps you find synergy through similarities while also honoring what makes you different. If you want to be an incredible salesperson, let the networks and best practices of your competition inform your sales approach. If you are a designer and want to express your visualization process better, then identify and mimic the styles that accomplished designers use when they introduce their creations to the world. Before creating your own signature dishes, learn the techniques and creative styles of other successful bakers, cooks, and chefs. Ultimately, this will allow you to discover your own style, and then you will flourish because of your understanding of what has made the greats great.

We see this all the time with high-performance athletes and accomplished artists and musicians. Often, they have spent years mastering the techniques and styles of the greats who came before them before forming their own path.

While it is important to be yourself and to eventually discover your own personal style and identity, it is absolutely critical to take advantage of the ability to shapeshift. This power will single-handedly make you one of the most attractive and relatable people in the room. It will strengthen your creative core. And it will empower you to be more confident in the initiatives you set out to accomplish.

Rehabilitation

The superpower of rehabilitation comes not only from the continuous growth of your creative core, but also from an attitude of resilience. I have found that this superpower requires dedication, focus, and an affirming belief that you have more to give to the world after a setback. Rehabilitation is a power that all superhumans choose to tap into at some point in their journey. Here's the secret of this superpower: if you can learn how to improve your own abilities after a loss, whether professionally or personally, you can show others how to rehabilitate as well. But to grow this superpower, I have found that you must hone it during the moments of defeat, when you experience deep loss of self-sufficiency.

In a span of three months, I went from making the highest income I'd ever made in my life to being unemployed, with no severance as a buffer. On top of this loss, I experienced one of the worst physical accidents in my life while playing basketball in a routine Saturday pickup game. Thinking I still had the strength and ability I did in my twenties, I foolishly tried to dunk. I landed awkwardly and at full velocity on my left leg and immediately went limp. I literally could not feel my leg.

Turns out I had completely blown my ACL and MCL, two of the four major ligaments in the knee. It would require an intensive surgery and months of physical therapy to regain a fraction of the mobility that I had prior to the injury. I had to work with several physical therapists just to learn how to walk again.

During this time, I realized that a resilient mindset that fights to *get back* to pursuing your overall potential in life after a big setback is, indeed, commendable. But at times, we will face challenges and setbacks greater that what we can overcome with our current thinking. Suffering a major injury can be one of those times. And working through the process of recovery in the right way can help us develop a new level of cognition and reach new heights of our potential.

This, then, is a power that requires defeat, failure, pain, and even setbacks at first. Imagine that: a superpower that requires you to experience something arguably negative and difficult before you can access it. It might seem counterintuitive, until you realize that life is full of many tough moments of personal loss, just as it is full of lovely, beautiful moments of growth. To live to your full potential, you will have to develop the ability to rehabilitate quickly and to grow from your experiences. And since these difficult, frustrating, and arduous times of loss in our lives are unavoidable, we will have to grow this superhuman ability stronger and further with every setback if we're to take advantage of the other superpowers we'll need to *do* more and *be* more.

What must you do to achieve this? Opening your deepest emotions and beliefs to experience your higher spiritual core will put you in the position to rehabilitate faster. This is what I call faith: believing in a better future after a setback or loss, even though you are facing a long road to recovery. Chasing what you cannot see may not feel rational. But faith will be the exact element necessary to push through our biggest personal failures, setbacks, and mistakes in order to grow toward our greater potential. My faith in God has been one of the most critical elements of my rehabilitation superpower. While I am not challenging you to accept my faith, I am asking you to think about when faith—particularly faith in a power beyond your own—has been the most meaningful to you.

To rehabilitate, you must believe that you can go beyond your current state. You must have faith that your audience of family and friends will help you back onto your course of purpose with compassion. You will also connect mind, body, and spirit in ways you never imagined possible. Talk with anyone who has recovered from serious loss: cancer, a major injury, the death of a loved one. Rehabilitation requires the greatest level of creativity. You must imagine new ways to be incredibly *conscious of*, or present with, the work of gaining strength. You must be *connected* deeply with those close to your cause and mission. And ultimately, you must be vulnerable and humble enough to experience the love and grace of a *community*.

Real rehabilitation also involves separating ourselves from the injury. Our human tendency is to absorb the failure, setbacks, and losses to the point that they become our entire identity. And this can become detrimental. As we pursue the path of becoming superhuman, we must also embrace the fact that we are still human and that sometimes we still make incredible mistakes.

I truly believe that God did not place us in this world to be the direct result of our failures, setbacks, and losses. Ultimately, even our worst and most painful moments are part of a bigger story that can add to the value of so many other individuals. To rehabilitate, we must separate our moments of brokenness from our true identity and embrace the bigger journey we are on to enrich the world. When we instead stay emotionally attached to the experience to the point where it begins to define us, it is all too easy to project this loss or brokenness onto other people. It becomes a barrier for us *and* for them.

I do not want this for you. I want you to go beyond that moment of loss. Don't absorb moments like these into your DNA. Don't let these losses eat at your creative core. Instead, put more energy into developing the possibilities of your future. What lives will you inspire by pushing to new heights despite the setback? What results could come about that shape the world to be a better place? As you rehabilitate, is there an opportunity to commit to a higher level of grace and beauty in your life?

BUILD YOUR OWN POWERS

The real power of living superhuman-by-design comes when you recognize that we all have access to superpowers.

Ultimately, the superpowers will be what you describe to others when they ask how you move forward with passion and purpose, living your life to the fullest. Remember, while it is great to grow your creative core and design ways to hone special abilities, we do it for the results—for the impact in our own lives and the lives of those around us.

Even if the superpowers listed in this chapter are not the ones you relate to the most, you can discover your own superpowers among the talents you already have. We will talk about that in the next chapter.

DON THE CAPE!

The superhero's cape has historical and cultural significance. For some superheroes, the cape accentuates their strength; for others, it serves as an element of their personality. Often the cape expresses a sense of power and majesty outside the reach of humanity. In some cases, it even serves as a weapon. Though Hollywood today often abandons the superhero cape, during the golden age of comics the vision was of caped crusaders. And those capes were distinctive and memorable. We can recognize a superhero by his or her cape, the one first created for them as emblematic of who they are in their fictional world.

Wonder Woman's cape is a reminder of her legacy of royalty from her home island of Themyscira. Batman and Superman, two of the earliest comic-book superheroes, are usually depicted with their iconic capes billowing majestically in the wind. These universal images have become the generic visual blueprint for what we think about when we imagine superheroes.

Each superhero's cape communicates something unique, as well as emphasizing a particular superhuman ability or set of abilities. The cape is a symbol and an announcement.

In much the same way, we are given elements that other people can identify us by. A personality trait that we are known for, perhaps, or a talent that is particularly ours. People tend to have at least one or two talents that are natural to them and with which they can do well. Unfortunately, most of us struggle to know what to do with the abilities we have. I want you to know that along with the superpowers you'll develop in practice, you already have within you incredible talents and qualities that can communicate inspiring energy to the world around you.

But first you have to pull back the metaphorical curtain blocking the sunlight that would illuminate the remarkable talents you already have. You can do this by embracing the unique and positive things that people already recognize about you. Embrace the fact that the talents you have offer you an advantage in every aspect of your life and also that they play a crucial role in growing your creative core. As you see opportunities to harness and focus your talents, along with new superpowers, you will see that you are capable of much more than you're doing right now.

I call this honest inventory of your natural abilities "donning (that is, putting on) the cape." Undertaking this inventory also means being honest about any self-induced distractions that keep you from living as you would like. Every day, we have an opportunity to "don the cape" by developing ourselves. The more we design daily ways of being creative, the more we will grow our natural abilities and develop our superpowers. As we do this, our superhuman lives will be evident, both to others and to ourselves, from the amazing and life-changing results we are delivering.

Superhumans wear their capes every day and approach the world with a simple question: "Is it impossible?" This is the mindset of someone who wants to *do* more and to *be* more for themselves and others. This is not to say that nothing will be impossible. Of course, there are a multitude of things that are completely out of our control. I am asking you to think about the impossible in terms of your mindset and to commit to accomplishing more than perhaps you think you can in this moment. Once you commit, you will be motivated to take the necessary steps to adopt a superhuman mindset.

As examples, you might ask yourself, is it *impossible* to achieve that degree? Is it *impossible* to develop a nutrition plan that helps your body reach a new level of well-being? Is it *impossible* to launch that new business venture? Donning the cape represents extending yourself beyond how you might previously have considered your talents or approached achieving your goals.

Now you can take an active role in developing your natural talent and superpowers with goals in sight. As superhumans, we see that by making our talent operable, our "capes" go into action and help us "fly" to new heights. Even more, as we develop our natural talents and grow our superpowers, we spread hope to others. By wearing our capes and creating value for others through our abilities, we can help others believe that they too will deliver something awe-inspiring to the world.

As we begin to redefine what's possible, we can also begin to understand the "why" behind living a superhuman life. Without understanding the "why," we are unable to fully embrace the commitment that this way of living requires of us. Without the "why," it is all too easy to dismiss the ideal of developing superpowers and to settle instead into living average lives that seek only comfort, self-fulfillment, and superficial success. From experience, I have learned that seeking comfort alone usually brings on a lack of fulfillment and a deep dissatisfaction with the tools I have been given. I challenge us instead to push aside any hesitancy about developing those talents and to wear our capes boldly and confidently.

The choice is ours. We have all been given gifts, abilities, and tools that enable us to reach toward our full potential and to seek to do the impossible in various areas of our lives.

Professionally, I wear the cape when I develop my natural talent of sketching with the superpower of teleportation. My creative ability is further strengthened because I approach the work in front of me with techniques and technologies that help me generate new and exciting images for clients. In the end, I create value and deliver game-changing results. Personally, I wear the cape when I decide to serve in the community. By developing my natural ability to communicate along with my superpower of shapeshifting, I am able to relate to the needs of others and teach in a way that is approachable and engaging.

To embrace being superhuman, take a moment at the start of each day to visualize how to make possible something that you are facing that seems impossible. Then, throughout the day, help others around you to ask themselves "Is it impossible?" and watch as people slowly become believers that something greater can be brought to life.

Many companies that we recognize as having successful brands and products have built entire creative cultures by asking questions around what is possible. Reimagining what could be accomplished will encourage you to look at your talents in a new light and to think of how to creatively develop and grow those talents to work in conjunction with your newfound superpowers.

Now, here's the pivot: asking whether something is truly impossible is only a prompt to get us thinking differently. From there, we must apply the tools that enable us to build a life to suit that different thinking.

Which takes us to the next step. By now, you should have a good feeling for the foundation of a superhuman-by-design life. You understand the importance of creativity to this life, and you know how to grow your creative core by applying the design process. You've also explored the significance of the Superhuman Code, which provides the guiding framework, and the superpowers, the life-altering abilities you'll use to accomplish what you accomplish.

But you have not yet learned how to look at your life squarely to determine where and how to apply everything you're absorbing about this new life where it will mean the most right now. You do not yet know how to design ways of mastering superpowers in every aspect of your life. For that, you need the Superhuman Pillars.

THE SUPERHUMAN PILLARS

The Superhuman Pillars are recommendations for growth in four key areas of your life: spirit and mind, fitness and health, finances, and relationships and people. I recommend reading about these recommendations and then thinking about how to apply them in your own life. That thinking is actually "ideating," and when you engage in this sort of thinking, you are working in the Ideating phase of the design process. Eventually, you will begin to prototype, or build out, the habits, practices, and strategies that serve you the best. Finally, you will begin to test what is helping you grow and develop. As the process becomes cyclical, you will begin to iterate more quickly and gain insights faster about the best ways to focus your natural abilities and the superpowers in various areas of your life. The superhuman-by-design process is satisfying because as you begin to try out these concepts, you will quickly discover what works and what doesn't. And you'll begin to see real results.

Each pillar includes thoughts and exercises for working through that pillar in your own life. The process of becoming and living superhuman will require you not to be delicate with the following pages! Plan to use this chapter as a workbook. Highlight the principles and recommendations that jump out at you. Then, begin to jot down notes about how you might fine-tune your thoughts and try new actions in your life. Do not underestimate the power of a highlighter and a notebook to capture your thoughts as you work through this process. Post-It Notes or any notes app on your phone or laptop can also be handy. Whatever works for you.

Each day in this journey you'll be throwing your full creative self into getting better at realizing your full potential. Each day offers a new canvas, a new opportunity.

SPIRIT AND MIND

From the Heart, the Mouth Speaks

One of the most transcendent moments of my life involved recognizing that my emotions and thoughts were deeply connected to my spiritual well-being. By spiritual well-being, I mean the immaterial aspect of yourself that gives you a sense of meaning and purpose in your life. Our minds are often influenced by our spiritual wellness, and it can be easy to neglect looking into the deeper connection between what we believe and our actions. I have come to understand that only through a sincere investigation into our spiritual well-being—that is, weighing the intentions of our hearts—can we begin to see new dimensions of the ourselves and gain a greater awareness of what we bring to the world. Only when we admit that we are more than mind, body, and emotions will we be able to live a life that is transformative, fulfilling, and brilliant. Our superhuman selves must understand that our spirits and minds are the gateways to living our greatest potential. And that spirit, that mind, and that heart are reflected in what we say.

There is a verse in the Bible that says,

> ***A good person produces good out of the good stored up in his heart. An evil person produces evil out of the evil stored up in his heart, for his mouth speaks from the overflow of the heart.***

In other words, whatever we have deeply embedded in our hearts, or the spiritual core of our being, is what we eventually release into the world. It is no mystery that our thoughts are critical to our vision for doing and being more in life. For this reason, one of the most important elements of the Superhuman Pillar of spirit and mind is understanding how what we say is an intimate reflection of our perspective on the world. It is the purest manifestation of what we believe.

And of all the things that we might say, confessing is a particularly pure and direct line from heart to mind. Some of the greatest and most influential leaders have changed the course of history and left legacies with what they shared from their hearts. For example, when we think about the American civil rights leader Dr. Martin Luther King, Jr., we are often awestruck by his speeches on racial injustice in America that were both emotionally inspiring and highly intellectual. In one of his sermon essays, he wrote about how tragic it is to have a gap between the high-value principles we profess and the low-integrity actions that often contradict those words. As Dr. King put it,

> ***One day we will learn that the heart can never be totally right if the head is totally wrong. This is not to say that the head can be right if the heart is wrong. Only through the bringing together of head and heart—intelligence and goodness—can man rise to a fulfillment of his true essence.***

I have come to see in my own life that if my heart and mind are misaligned, I cannot do the work of achieving a new and more fulfilled existence. If you are ignoring the bridge between heart and mind, there are untapped strengths and talents in you right now. You are unfulfilled.

What you say directly reflects what you believe: it is a reflection of where your heart and your thoughts are in this moment.

Knowing Who You Are

One of the greatest achievements of any life journey is to understand what makes you, you.

Whether we begin by listening to those around us or by undertaking our own journey of self-discovery and introspection, we are all trying to make sense of who we are and what purpose we serve in the world.

Our inner being wants that. We want to be more in the world. We want more than a humdrum, mediocre life. The superhuman effect reminds that even by small actions we can have a significant impact on others around us throughout our lives. As we take action to learn more about ourselves, we take steps forward in living superhuman. The practices we undertake in our lives right now are a reflection of what drives our thoughts and our will. Is it our ego, our insecurities, our pride, our desire for comfort? What motivates us, in fact, when we set out to discover what we value the most? These things are important to explore because you can then begin to see the connection between what you value and the identity you inhabit.

The key is to adopt an open, courageous mindset when seeking to understand more clearly who you are and then being honest about the parts of your identity you need to address. For me, I had to take "inventory" of my identity and look at my belief system and the things motivating my actions in the world. I thought I knew who I was until I begin to diagnose habits in my life that were not giving me healthy, positive thoughts or generating value for others. As I embraced the journey of being superhuman, I designed margin, or time, into each day to reflect deeply on whether I was becoming a more inspiring, uplifting, and positive person—or whether I was instead becoming a more self-serving, ego-driven person. It sounds simple, and for the most part it is, but it requires consistency and an understanding that your identity is shaped by your mindset.

At the end of this section is a "Call to Creativity," which offers some creative methods to help you design ways to recognize who you are today and then to think about who you want to be going forward. We get to choose whether or not to exploit the power of our creative core and take a step forward in designing ways to explore our personal growth.

You Were Created to Be Creative

If our superheroes only concentrated on declaring who they are, they would miss out on the practical application of their gifts. I would argue that we were created to be creative. This is not meant to be a stumbling block, as

I understand that some of you reading this book might object to a Christian-centric worldview founded on the concept of "being created."

But what I often tell people is that our view of our identity plays a big part in how we engage our creative selves. As you explore your identity and learn more about yourself, I want you to recognize that you can create value and purpose, in your life and in the world. This is a holistic view of our identity, a perspective that emphasizes a connection between whom we believe we are and what we believe we can create. Our creative expressions and explorations can be a deeper reflection of our mindset and state of spiritual wellness. In fact, I have found that when I feel confident about who I am, I am generally more intuitive and creative.

I truly believe that the most heroic and superhuman actions we can take during our time on this earth are to create value and purpose for ourselves and others. Through my professional and personal experiences over the past several years, I have found that my greatest fulfillment comes when I am approaching each day creatively and imagining new ways to inspire and help other people. When I live this way, I recognize that I am giving hope to the world.

Think about moments when you were creative or when you created an intention and pursued it strategically. What were the results? Did you feel fulfilled? Did you experience a new level of satisfaction? Have you ever helped a neighbor, a classmate, or a child with a problem by offering up a creative solution and then seen the resulting glow of happiness or glint of excitement?

Asking yourself questions such as these enables you to take a step forward in the superhuman journey and discover more about the underlying motivations that form your identity. As a superhuman, I live for the moments when I imagine a new possibility for my own life or create value in the life of someone else. At the end of the metaphorical day, you are not evaluated by your position or your material gain. You are evaluated by whether you are leaning into your creative core and bringing your novel, unique self to the world.

Call to Creativity

Actions for Exploring the Superhuman Pillar of Spirit and Mind

- → Travel to the most sacred and beautiful places of worship in the world. Spend time learning how these places of worship were used in their particular cultures and meditating on them. Take photos, sketch, or journal at these sites.

- → Submit any of your creative work for a greater cause, contest, or innovation award. Or participate in creating a community mural, and while there, talk with others about their reasons for contributing to the project.

- → Write down what you are passionate about and spend time journaling about what makes your perspective unique. You can also do this by generating a Pinterest board of images that represent your passions.

- → Find outlets through your offline and online communities to submit original work. This can be anything from your hobbies to the works you create through collective community interests. It does not matter if it is game design, poetry, basket weaving, or making fishing lures. Leverage social media to find a group that is generally positive and productive.

- → Track how much time you dedicate each month to creative pursuits. Also, remember that your confidence to explore the Superhuman Pillars will be fueled by your daily access to the superpowers you are developing.

FITNESS AND HEALTH

Think about how busy your life is right now.

The demands, the schedules, the emails, the travel. Even if you are in a stage of life that affords you more flexibility in how you spend your time, think about how quickly the day can slip by when not intentionally designed for your maximum productivity. Our productivity depends on our energy and the steps we take to renew that energy. We all know that our energy affects our moods and emotions—which ultimately influences how creative we are throughout the day.

And this is why the pillar of fitness and health is so important. Our desire to *do* more and to *be* more can dominate our time. We need a creative approach to fitness and well-being that empowers us to keep going even when we can find a million reasons to leave the superhuman path. So, if you are living superhuman-by-design, maintaining your fitness and health is key for staying true to your path and achieving your goals, no matter the busyness and challenges that life might bring.

Now, a couple of definitions. When I refer to "fitness," I am talking about getting creative with the activities that stimulate positive outcomes in your body. When I refer to "health," I am highlighting the overall, holistic approach we must all take to our well-being—physical, mental, and emotional. As we aim to function at optimal levels, we will need to think creatively about designing rhythms and rituals in our lives that help us accomplish great things and avoid burnout.

The hardest part is taking the first step. Wherever we begin, whatever transition we're looking to make, we can use the design process to experiment and get creative with our health. You do not have be Serena Williams or the Rock to see incredible transitions for the better in terms of your overall health, your lifestyle, or your body. You just have to adopt the superhuman-by-design approach, which leverages your creative core. As you review the details of this pillar, remember that the outcomes of every step you take will be inspirational and informative for others. You aren't going to just look like a superhuman and feel like one. You are also going to influence others to live a higher-quality life.

Be the Creative Producer of Your Healthier Self

As recently as 2017, I was what many people would consider a relatively healthy individual. I tried to maintain a weekly exercise routine; I went for checkups; I managed my diet and nutrition; I even tried to use apps and smart devices to track my sleep and meditation time.

But when I tore my ACL in a freak basketball accident, I spent over six months recovering from the injury and subsequent surgery. During that time, my entire body changed and many of my former practices went right out of the window. I began to read more about trainers who had built up star-studded lists of clients through their creative social media feeds. Some of these men and women had advanced degrees in physiology and nutritional sciences and emphasized holistic approaches to health and wellness. The trainers would often post short videos showing their daily stretch routines, yoga sessions, or high-intensity workouts. It did not matter whether they were in a hotel room, their backyard, or even outside in a park—they revealed to me that I did not have to go to the gym to achieve another level of fitness. I also learned a lot about the human body in terms of how to increase my oxygen level and improve my digestion.

The creativity of some of these modern celebrity and social media trainers sparked my new perspective on fitness and health. Their videos became the mental and emotional fuel for my recovery process. In their YouTube videos and Instagram profiles, they went past the glitz of a trim, spray-tanned body and focused on comprehensive approaches to taking care of the body and mind despite fitness level or schedule. I have shared a few fitness resources in the notes to this chapter as points of departure. Part of the creativity of engaging with online teachers is that often they are independent and looking for their own creative ways to make fitness activities and nutrition more interesting for others.

The key is to become the creative producer of the methods and activities that inspire you to be a healthier you. Adopt the routines and activities that you can weave into your life based on your constraints of space and time. Focus on making incremental advancements in your knowledge of your health and maximize your productive time by aligning with trainers who are empathetic to the same constraints. For instance, I often found that working out with a video from a yoga instructor doing a fifteen-minute video in her home encouraged me to try a different session daily, without the requirement of traveling to a studio and feeling like a newbie. For me, *Yoga Journal* has been a valuable resource.

In the end, everyone around you benefits, and you will also bring your most superhuman self to the world much faster. People notice when a person is doing a great job with their overall health and fitness. You will beam with energy and passion. You'll have a "glow" about you that tells the world you are taking an active, holistic approach to health and wellness.

As the creative producer of health and wellness in your life, you can choose the time of day that you are most motivated, or able, to be active. I encourage you to think less about the things hindering you from considering your health and wellness. Instead, get creative about what might inspire you to take care of yourself more and then design plans to try it. Whether unplugging from all your tech and going for a long walk or challenging your muscles through in-home exercises with a resistance band and full-body workout routines, you can increase your fitness level and improve your overall well-being. If you want to take advantage of the technology available, you can leverage your personal device by setting it to "Do Not Disturb" and then using it to go through an online workout routine or one of the meditation sessions offered on an app like Calm.

If you're creative with your breaks and manage your snacking, you'll find that even small changes can pay huge dividends, most particularly during your busiest seasons. You'd be surprised how much you can get done with relatively little time when you design your breaks to maximize your ability to recover and recharge. I often layer my physical workouts with mental breaks to breathe, stretch, and even meditate to cool down. As you learn your body's needs, you can choose to decrease your overall sugar intake and increase the amount of water you drink between meetings and calls.

Again, the overall goal is to recognize that *you* are the creative producer of your health and wellness, meaning that you have the power to design simple, daily approaches to taking care of yourself. Experiment with what works best for you.

Learn the Art of Creative Destruction

Creative destruction involves taking intentional steps to remove the elements from your life that are no longer serving your overall health and well-being. By doing this, we create margin, or room, for better things to come into our lives.

The path to becoming superhuman in your health requires an attitude that seeks to dismantle the traditional and accepted ideas of what works and what doesn't. For instance, it is widely accepted that going to a gym is your ticket to a better body. But over time, I have learned that there are alternative environments, such as outdoor workout parks, that can offer new experiences in developing your overall health and wellness.

Again, being superhuman-by-design in areas of health and fitness is not so much about achieving those perfectly sculpted abs as much as it is about structuring elements into our lives that help us deliver our most effective and energetic selves to the world each day.

That said, it is important to understand that what we leave behind or take away can be just as critical as what we add. In the design world, we call this *reductive design.*

This type of design practice has a basis in minimalism, and it asks designers to analyze the components of a design and then to get rid of anything that competes with the design goals.

Well-known designers work hard to make sure both that a user interface has only what users need and that it does not cause confusion. In much the same way, we must approach our overall health through fitness and nutrition, by determining exactly what we need when we need it. So much of what traps us has to do with the comforts of our personal world.

Eating at fast-food restaurants or snacking on whatever we can quickly order or access, though convenient, enforces unhealthy habits. Engaging with social media can siphon away the precious time and energy we have to do more in our lives. Unhealthy habits like these carry a high cost, because they drain the focus and stamina we need for the tasks that require us to be our best selves. Examine what elements you can and should remove from your life. This can begin with the unhealthy foods in your pantry and extend into other areas of your life that impact your overall health.

Case in point: over the course of the past year, I managed to keep my cell phone out of my bedroom before sleeping. I reduced my need and desire to read through news, social media, or LinkedIn late at night. I then added an Amazon Kindle and Bluetooth headphones into my new bedtime routine. Now I can spend the final fifteen to twenty minutes of my day reading on a display that does not hurt my eyes while listening to calm, meditative music. This change in routine has drastically improved my sleep patterns and helped me to be much more productive during the day.

Another creative-destruction moment became evident to me when I started training consistently but noticed that many of the sports drinks I consumed after the workout were high in sugar. As I paid attention to other superhumans who were conscious of the fuel they put into their bodies both pre- and post-workout, it became clear to me that many of them drank water with electrolytes. The more I learned about the importance of adequate hydration, the more I explored creative, cost-effective ways to have this water available before and after working out. Since that realization, I have avoided the aisle at the store that contained all those sugary sports drinks.

Practice the "Two Are Better than One" Principle

Given the obstacles we often face daily in balancing the divergent demands of our lives, we may find that partnering with someone else can be instrumental in our fitness and wellness. Though I have found times of isolation necessary so as to focus on achieving a specific fitness goal, I have benefited tremendously from having a partner on my journey.

If you choose to work with a professional trainer or nutritionist, you might be able to chart your progress more easily. Either way, choosing a workout partner can open the door to sustaining a lifestyle of fitness and wellness. Over the years, I have discovered that working out with a friend has not only increased the effectiveness of my workouts but also, and more importantly, has enhanced my overall attitude toward wellness.

I saw my first example of the power of this strategy while at Kettering University. During my freshman year, I met a classmate who was out of shape but had an uncanny ability to keep his commitments. Over the course of a few months of getting to know him, I noticed that he remained committed to our study sessions no matter what else was going on.

Every day, we would meet in the library for an hour to review the work to be completed. I eventually started inviting him to work out with me at the campus fitness center. I was looking for a way to stay in shape during the harsh Michigan winters, in which it was common to have a foot of snow on the ground for months.

My buddy was courageous enough to join me, and we began going to the fitness center every morning at six o'clock. Over the course of several weeks, we began to feel a connection as early risers who did not want to let the other person down by skipping a session.

The benefits for both of us over the course of a few months were astounding. We performed with increasing levels of intensity, and I began to actually see my buddy's body and mental focus transform. The time for our one-mile run continued to drop, and we were able to move with more flexibility, agility, and explosive strength in our exercise activities.

Meanwhile, I became healthier at an entirely new level. Not only was my conditioning at peak performance, but I also started seeing the benefits of nurturing my overall physical well-being. In addition to being able to easily run a 10K, I noticed a boost in my energy throughout the day as I juggled multiple classes and on-campus work.

So, my encouragement for those on the journey of becoming superhuman is to design ways that invite partnerships and community into your transition to greater physical well-being. At the end of the day, we are all challenged with finding time to achieve more during the week. But if we lean into the partnership model—in essence, the principle that two are better than one—we will be more consistent in sticking with our training, and most importantly, we will move past accepting mediocrity. Avoid any self-defeating thoughts, such as that it's too late for you to see big changes in your health, and find others around you who believe the same and who support your mission. Once you find a supportive community or the other half of your superhuman dynamic duo, just watch how much more productive you'll become over the course of a few months.

Call to Creativity

Actions for Exploring the Superhuman Pillar of Fitness and Health

→ If you are able-bodied, sign up for some form of physical competition. I have signed up for 5Ks and 10Ks, and doing so forced me to put a date on the board and to begin getting in shape and into a better state of wellness. It also often encouraged me to put the word out to friends and people in my community, opening the doors for new dynamic duos.

→ Adopt exercise programs that increase your tolerance and appetite to be the best you can be. In other words, just as many of us cannot absorb an entire school semester of a subject in a couple of classes, starting any nutrition and wellness discipline requires taking small steps and increasing the constraints over time. So, while cutting all sugar from your diet overnight might be an extreme step, can you track your eating habits for a full week to get a better feel for how much sugar (or other unhealthy items) you are consuming?

→ Accept that there are some hard rules. Here's a hard rule for all of us: gravity. What goes up will come down. Jump off a ten-foot ladder and you must deal with the consequences. It is the same with developing an attitude of wellness in our lives. Create the difference in your life between hard no's and soft no's. The hard no's become your hard rules. You don't budge on them. These are the obligations that dictate your wellness progress and that over time make you more effective. Here's an example: I have a hard rule of being in bed for a designated number of hours a night, four nights a week. Even if I am not able to stay asleep for all of those hours, I don't budge on that element of my wellness. An example of a soft no would be adhering to a diet but allowing yourself to occasionally have a "cheat day," during which you can enjoy your favorite high-calorie snack.

→ Incorporate moments of meditation into high-energy daily practices. For instance, when you transition from your commute into work or finish up an intense workout, designate five to ten minutes to meditate, breathe, and/or pray to come into a place of focus and mindfulness.

→ Practice your fitness in an environment of creativity and inspiration. Remember how people used to walk inside shopping malls to get their steps in? Well, my modern version of it is getting steps in at a museum of modern art, a spacious art garden with lots of stairs, or an architecture tour. Even weekly, I will choose a destination featuring something that inspires me and plan how to make it part of my "move" goals for that day.

→ Experiment with meditative physical activities that encourage you to move while also developing mental focus. Try various practices of yoga, martial arts, or hiking to see if there is a physical routine that gives you time to think and reflect while also moving your body.

FINANCE

What can superhumans reveal to us about finances?

Well, let's take another lighthearted look at our caped crusaders for some inspiration.

Think about it this way: if heroes like Iron Man or Batman were concerned only about their billion-dollar accounts, would they be free to serve the greater good? In fact, these characters are even more fascinating because though they are connected to a history of wealth, they choose to apply their intellect, resources, and will to saving others.

In the case of Batman, he chooses to live a life beyond the boardroom of Wayne Enterprises, applying his wit and energy to cleaning up Gotham.

Tony Stark, a witty and industrious genius who later becomes Iron Man, stands on the shoulders of his father, Howard Stark, a brilliant entrepreneur who built his wealth via Stark Industries, a weapons technology business. In Marvel's first *Iron Man* movie, we watch Tony explore his interests, which he is free to do because of the wealth he has through Stark Industries. Ultimately, though, his explorations put him in a position to save the lives of many people.

What about the T'Challa, the Black Panther? If he does not leverage his wealth and financial resources as the leader of a free kingdom, won't others lose in his society? Throughout his story, his leadership is illustrated by how he invests in the infrastructure, stability, and future of his nation, Wakanda.

These superheroes share an important characteristic: freed from financial pressure, they have embraced lives of purpose, driven by mission. They are depicted as larger-than-life, more-than-human characters who give society their best, no matter the challenges. Notably, one of those challenges is not money. But granted freedom from that pressure, they have not chosen a life of comfort. They have instead chosen one of struggle and strife.

While these are just superhero characters, their narratives reflect our craving for more than monetary success. Money is necessary, yes, but it is not the goal. We can accomplish so much more in life if we can free ourselves of the traps that chasing financial success can lock us into. True enough, I am supportive of taking responsibility for growing wealth and gaining financial freedom, but as superhumans, we are designing a higher-level purpose for that independence. The payoff of a superhuman-by-design life in your finances is not only increasing assets, but also being able to maximize your purpose and satisfaction in life, full-time, beyond the pitfalls of consumerism and status-quo mediocrity that demands security.

So, let's look at the means for unlocking the path to being superhuman-by-design in our finances.

Design a Mindset of Financial Freedom

As a newly minted engineer at Delphi and Safety back in 2007, all I could think about was how much money I could save in one year. I would sometimes daydream about what my salary could be once I moved up to the senior management levels of the company.

You see, I do not come from generational wealth. There were no millionaires in my family, and financial literacy when I was growing up was composed of whatever I learned at home about debt management and paying bills on time.

Once out of school, I thought employment at a top engineering company would be my ticket to a life of wealth. So I kept working hard. I earned promotions, took on new roles, and eventually found myself in the Bay Area working at a manager level making over six figures a year.

In time, I began to recognize that chasing higher salaries and bonuses, all while accumulating money for the purposes of security and status, was actually a lot easier to fall into than resist. Slowly, my desire to gain more meant longer and longer work hours and dealing with more corporate gatekeepers who curtailed my progress upward in the company. In a desire to free myself from the slow-burn career of a nine-to-five corporate role, I decided to try to call more of the shots. I started making quick, impetuous moves to gain more independence and to make more money faster.

In fact, some of my most regrettable decisions financially have involved jumping at seemingly more lucrative opportunities only to find out that I was still not satisfied and still searching for freedom.

What followed was a period of time between late 2016 and most of

2017 in which I owned, worked, and managed my own business. While I did experience some sense of autonomy and a corporate independence with my company, Forecast Studios, I did not fully understand my motivation for becoming my own boss.

In my case, starting my own agency was a step in the right direction for more freedom and financial success. But I fell short in not having a vision for the endgame. I did not think about how my business could eventually transform into a scalable enterprise that would give me more opportunities. It was all about making fast money and feeding the ego by being an entrepreneur when it was socially popular.

That's when a superhuman truism hit me: it's not about a mindset locked on earning more, it's about a mindset locked on creating value for others. By design, I started digesting more and more material that instructed me on how to go beyond just getting my financial house in order and managing growing investments. I read more books on developing streams of passive income by leveraging my gifts, my talent, and the resources at my disposal. In building Forecast, I learned that financial independence really comes through creating opportunities for others, especially my employees. The more successful and fulfilled my creative team was, the more projects we won and the more income we made.

As superhumans, we empower ourselves by designing lives that free us up to invest more time and energy into the dreams and visions of others around us. If we can commit to creating wealth with the intention of having more time and energy both to pursue our dreams and to serve others, we supercharge our capability to live a fulfilled life that goes beyond the humdrum of chasing higher salaries. At this stage, I am still building toward complete financial freedom, but my mindset to do this and the activities related to bringing this reality to life are by design, not by default.

The "Call to Creativity" at the end of this section presents various ways to generate passive income, which is only part of the path to financial freedom. The real work comes in adjusting your mindset to think differently from the traditional perspectives that tell you to put your adventures and passions aside until retirement.

Supercharge an Attitude of Expectancy

One of the strongest parallels between fictional superheroes and real-life superhumans is their boundless expectancy that outcomes will work in their favor.

In fact, I think that these are the stories we remember the most from the movies. You can probably think of a couple of movies now where the main protagonist of the story seems to have absolutely everything working against them and then experiences an unbelievable stretch of achievement that just seems extraordinary. These are stories that move us.

One of my favorite movies in this genre is *The Pursuit of Happyness*, based on the true story of Chris Gardner. In the film, Gardner, who works as a salesman, struggles to support himself, his wife, and their son on his meager salary. His life is hard, filled with frustrations and disappointment. Despite his difficulties, he pursues an opportunity to become a stockbroker at a well-known brokerage. The opportunity comes at a high cost, as Gardner in his role as an unpaid intern has to compete with Ivy League graduates. We see that he is highly intelligent, every bit their equal, but his days are full of bad breaks and financial instability. His unpaid internship complicates his already fraught relationship with his wife, his bank account is garnished by the IRS, and at one point he loses one of the bone scanners he is supposed to be selling to pay the rent. Eventually, he becomes a single parent and is occasionally homeless. The low point is when Gardner and his son can find no room in the homeless shelters and are forced to stay in a restroom at a BART train station overnight.

Through all of this, Gardner never loses his superhuman attitude of expectancy. He never doubts his skill. He knows that landing an internship at the brokerage will change his life trajectory, and so he creates every avenue possible to prepare for the exams and interviews that will get him through the door. Not only does he become more efficient, but he also outdoes himself and all the other interns by taking a leap of faith in reaching out to people who could help him on his path. He maximizes his client contacts and profits by designing ways to make phone sales calls more efficiently. His desperation drives him to be as creative as possible in achieving his dreams and pushes him to design systems in his life that will allow him to pursue those dreams with all his might.

Here's what I am suggesting: nurturing an attitude of expectancy can be the fuel for your strategy of creating financial freedom. This is not about increasing your net worth to beat the status quo. This is about believing that investing the time and energy into your ideas and interests can lead to game-changing, life-changing results in the future. As we design our lives to get our income growing for us, we also are generating expectancy around a superhuman life filled with more opportunities and life choices.

We can supercharge this attitude of expectancy by choosing the right fuel to power this superhuman growth. The right fuel comes from your creative core. Engaging your passions, your talent, and your target audience are all part of the formula for generating this fuel.

In this endeavor, the 3 C's of Creativity—consciousness, connectivity, and community—are the elements that bring our best creative self forward. Your audience is your community, and if you deliver value to them through your passion and your talent, your projects will be in high demand and will eventually generate income. In fact, this community will become the source of the power that supercharges your attitude of expectancy because they will echo the desire for your ideas to succeed in the marketplace. This principle works outside of your professional career as well. With an attitude of expectancy, you can generate stunning results for your local community, nonprofit organizations doing good things in the world, and even your local faith organization.

Look for opportunities to increase your attitude of expectancy in every aspect of your finances. It could be through exploring entrepreneurial ideas or joining social-good projects that invest in the community. You can also explore a number of different apps, such as Robinhood and Acorns. These apps offer lots of educational videos, emails, lectures, and other online resources to help you learn more about investing in the good to generate wealth over time. As you begin to have greater expectations about your projects, you will see new ways to galvanize your best creative self and accelerate your financial independence.

The Rich Don't Get Rich Alone

There is one passion I wish I had connected with sooner: investing in people. Investing represents the link between being superhuman in our finances and being superhuman in our personal relationships. It is the mirror that shows us exactly how we value the treasure that we have in our lives. Investing reflects what we value the most, and it also reflects our attitude toward expectancy. One of the most valuable lessons I have learned is that every superhuman must invest in a worthy cause. Not only in the typical opportunities for financial growth, but also in people.

This is critical. No one I know who is a millionaire and who has the financial freedom to pursue their purpose full-time has done it alone. They have learned how to invest in people by adding value to their lives, and they have learned how to invest their time in learning from others who have successfully navigated their finances over the years.

As we invest in people—serving others, donating our caring spirit and expectant attitude—we will see them respond with trust. Trust will open the doors for collaboration and creativity. Trust can encourage two different individuals to invest in each other's businesses. Trust can lead to friends and family contributing money to your own endeavors. Trust can also open the doors to new information that relates directly to financial success. Over the years, as I have gained the trust of wealthy tech investors, I have found more success in raising capital for my own creative ventures. But people do this every day by fulfilling online orders on websites like Etsy and even on social media accounts. Often, these entrepreneurs get rich through their community, a community they have grown by way of investing time in giving insights to others.

In the end, what we invest in and how we invest is what really determines how superhuman of a life we have lived, a point canvassed more fully in the next chapter. For now, let's consider ways that we can invest to produce life-changing results.

Call to Creativity

Actions for Exploring the Superhuman Pillar of Finance

→ Try out financial planning and investment apps that also give you tools to learn and experiment on their platforms. Apps such as Robinhood, Acorns, and Mint are ways to proactively experiment with investing and managing your finances. The apps provide information that can be helpful in experimenting with a variety of savings models, portfolio investment styles, and debt-management strategies.

→ Entrepreneurialism is the fastest way to stoke your creative core as it pertains to finances. The immediate goal is not to make money and become rich from starting a business. Instead, experiment with something you love creating or with a service that brings you joy and helps others; that is a great way to explore what could ultimately be a business venture. Eventually, you might see an opportunity to monetize your hobby and create a way to generate recurring revenue. First, start with exploring what you are passionate about the most.

→ Learn how to maximize the concept of a "spin-off." Traditionally, a spin-off is a business term meant to describe an incidental result of a larger business line. We hear about them all the time—mostly in terms of products that employees have devised while working on a larger initiative. Pay attention to things in your life that might be worth a lot to others but that happen to be incidental things from your day-to-day life. For instance, your code hack might be a huge solution for businesses, or your doodles might be a very valuable illustration pack to an online community. Create demand with others by occasionally offering things they value.

→ Keep learning. There are plenty of blog articles, e-books, podcasts, and honest social media channels that regularly offer novel, creative approaches to managing your finances, growing your investments, and starting a business. Leverage these resources and absorb the information. You can create a ritual of absorbing this information by integrating it with other recharge rituals, such as taking a walk or going on a long drive.

RELATIONSHIPS AND PEOPLE

Find Your Tribe

It is often said that your inner circle plays a huge part in your success. When I started out, the evidence of this truth became clear very quickly. I attribute this to the fact that I spent time around people who were older than me and further along in their lives and their careers.

But here is what I did not realize at the time: it's not just about finding the right group of people for your inner circle, it's about growing closer with those within that inner circle who want to accomplish extraordinary things in life. It's about deepening and strengthening relationships with individuals within the circle until you find something I call your "tribe."

Let me explain this process further and why it is a key to becoming superhuman-by-design.

When I started college in 2003, I was like many kids entering their freshman year: alone, looking to make new friends, and trying to stay in touch with friends I had grown up with who were at other schools. What revolutionized this experience for my generation was the explosion of "The Facebook" in 2004. And yes, in 2004, it was still called The Facebook.

The social media platform was humble and small in those days—only a handful of schools across the country were on the network. But throughout my college career, I watched as Facebook became arguably one of the most defining companies of the twenty-first century. My entire day seemed wrapped around looking at the posts of friends I had grown up with, checking in on the lives of new people I was interested in, and reading my feed for comments and likes. It was absolutely addicting. Even more, I could not help but add more and more people to my network. Eventually, I had thousands of "friends," and I would often feel overwhelmed by the proliferation of alerts in my inbox apprising me of their life updates.

Ultimately, it began to change how I made friends in real life. As a more introverted high schooler, I would make friendships slowly and look for people who were on the same wavelength in terms of their creative curiosity about the world. But with Facebook, I became emboldened in real life to seek out people who were living lives that I perceived to be more appealing and glamorous.

Throughout my twenties after college I watched as the numbers continued to go up in my social network and my circles expanded. I still followed the lives of people I had grown up with and even the new friends from college, but I also seemed to spend a lot of time mining for new relationships. I even started to do this on new platforms that emerged, like Instagram, Twitter, and LinkedIn. The question of quality versus quantity did not arise for me because everyone was trying to connect online.

But once I started moving further into my career and personal growth, I realized that I was doing myself a huge disservice. It actually dawned on me while catching up with a good friend whom I had not seen in years. During our lunch, all I could do was constantly chat about all of these new people in my life, to the point that I was not focused on what he was sharing about his own. It was a turning point.

It wasn't that connecting with lots of people and expanding my circles was a negative thing; it was just that I had not paid attention to deepening my relationships with the people who were closest to me. These people had seen my growth and still wanted me to accomplish more, they had stood by me as I made mistakes, and they had influenced me through their own desires to go to the next level. These friends, mentors, and relatives were not just in my inner circle, they were the right people in my inner circle: my tribe.

The tribe forms when you deepen your relationships with a handful of people who are in your inner circle. In other words, you might have people who are in your inner circle because you love them and care for them deeply, but who may not be pushing you to do more with your life. Forming your tribe is not about necessarily cutting these people out of your life. Often, these people might be family or coworkers you have been around for years. They are not going anywhere anytime soon, and you may spend lots of time and energy growing your relationships with them.

In contrast, the people you select from this inner circle to form your tribe are the people you need in order to succeed in accomplishing your visions and dreams. The inner circle can help you steer your life toward big, superhuman outcomes, and they can help you create viable strategies for moving forward even when you experience failure. Superhumans deeply understand the value of forming a tribe, and they design systems into their lives that foster the strengthening of their inner circle. More often than not, superhumans will prioritize the long-term fulfillment that comes from patiently developing tight bonds with a handful of people rather than putting tons of energy into amassing a huge network of names and faces.

Think about it this way: there are many superhero groups that come together with the purpose of accomplishing great things. The X-Men, for instance, are mutants who form a tight inner circle of sometimes-hero characters who strive for peace and equality between normal humans and mutants in a world where anti-mutant bigotry is rampant.

One of the most standout aspects of this group of Marvel characters is the story line following the tightening and strengthening of their relationships. Not only do they unite on bringing good to humanity and equality for other mutants, but they also understand that in order to achieve this goal they must go deeper in their trust and care for one another.

In much the same way, I have learned that to become superhuman-by-design, you must go deep emotionally with a handful of individuals in your inner circle and establish a tribe.

Being self-reliant and doing it yourself can only take you so far. Building an inner circle is great, but it can be regressive if you are merely staying close to people who neither challenge your fears nor instigate creative thinking through their questions and feedback. So, in order to chase your potential, spend more effort and time shaping your tribe and tightening your relationships with these individuals.

Live an Inspired Life

You have probably heard of TED talks—short, inspirational videos of conference talks by speakers who are innovators or experts in their fields. I encourage everyone reading this book to find time each week to listen to a TED talk because they invite audiences to think about new, creative concepts. As a professional designer, I am always looking for concepts that inspire me and give me new ideas.

One TED talk that has deeply affected me was given by Carol Dweck, a well-known psychologist and professor at Stanford University. She often speaks to audiences about a "growth mindset." The growth mindset is chock-full of insightful elements, each building on the basic concept that your qualities are important pieces of you that can be cultivated through your efforts. The growth mindset can also give you a creative lens through which you can frame failures and leverage them for future success.

One of my favorite quotes from Dweck is "Becoming is better than being." Her TED talk has challenged me to think about my own motivations and the reasons behind why I have become more attracted to people with progressive mindsets.

Over time I realized that I want not only to be inspired by people but also to live an inspired life that motivates others.

Superhumans don't just look to be inspired—though that is an important part of progressing toward a superhuman life. They work hard at being the people whom others are inspired by in their own daily lives. If superhumans are in the room where big decisions are being made, they influence the results that come out of that room for good. Too often, we leverage our creativity for self-serving activities that involve always putting our priorities over the priorities of others. In the end, we leave no room for our creativity to work in our personal and professional lives to make sizeable, impactful changes in the world around us.

Think about the selfless coaches, mentors, and teachers whom you might have met on your life journey. What made them stand out? What did they have in common? One important aspect was that they were probably invested in your success. Here's the bottom line: we are inspired by others who we sense are there for our greater good. Why? Because they want us to go beyond just "being" and to become the best versions of ourselves. We are also inspired by these superhumans because they create psychological and physical safe places for us to express our fears and hopes. By creating such spaces, these individuals open doors for honest, healthy dialogue and creative explorations of how to move things forward.

The key to becoming more superhuman with people is to begin demonstrating that you are invested in the success of others around you. Eventually, you will notice how others become more motivated to accomplish goals in their own lives because you are invested in seeing them reach those new heights.

While leading the team at Skully, I discovered how important it was to inspire people to do things that they never imagined they could do. I also discovered how important it was for me to keep pushing with a lot of enthusiasm at ways to accomplish what seemed impossible. More often than not, we lacked the budget to do big marketing campaigns. So we had to be scrappy. As the leader of the creative team, I had to be scrappy. For me, learning how to be scrappy took me out of my comfort zone; especially because I had previously been working in the plush confines of a multimillion-dollar company.

Every day, I figured out a way to inspire people through my enthusiasm and action-oriented energy. Sometimes this looked like editing some of our content or writing some copy for our website. I took the team to quick offsites at lunch and gave everyone the room to express their opinions about how we could market the product better through our social channels. I found ways to communicate the value of everyone on my team and led inspiration sessions for people to talk about their passions and interests. By leading these activities, I showed the team that no one was excluded from the process of bringing something great to our cohort. Slowly, it started working. People felt my conviction and believed that we were advancing. They felt included in the mission to build a big fan base for the brand, and they saw their efforts translate into growth.

My desire was to become the person in the room who motivated everyone to build stuff that was exciting and cool, without going out and hiring agencies. In the end, the team began to feel that nothing was too outlandish or too big to pull off, and our passion spread through the company.

Over the course of just a couple of months, the results of our scrappy marketing campaigns resounded so well that even big motorcycle brands like Ducati began to take notice and retweet and repost our ads! Once I began pointing out these positive outcomes, it built my confidence and credibility and made me that much hungrier to do more. Everyone took notice, and soon others began to say something I had not heard before in my interactions with others: "Donald, you inspire me!"

You can do the same in your professional and personal life for your coworkers, friends, and family. Even for your neighbors! Living an inspired life encourages others to imagine possibilities for their own lives and in turn paves the way to more meaningful relationships.

Share the Knowledge

Here's a word that you won't be able to escape regardless of whether the superhuman concept hits home or not: *leadership*. Leadership is one of the most-searched words on the web, and now more than ever it is studied as one of the key pillars to the success of any endeavor.

I am still on a path of learning how to be a leader and how to show leadership in every area of my life. Leadership is a lifelong endeavor that is often strengthened by the situations we live through over the course of our lives. It is an alchemy of many ingredients, especially the values I have outlined in the chapter on the Superhuman Code. There are many of us who are pushed into leadership through professional or life circumstances and others who seek opportunities to be out in front, leading the action. Whatever the reason, when you find yourself in a moment with the power to guide the outcome, recognize that this is when your superhuman leadership is needed the most.

Superhuman leaders practice sharing their knowledge, and in turn they build strong, game-changing relationships with people. Whether it is sharing knowledge through effective, transparent communication with others or sharing knowledge through platforms, superhumans find a way to pass along what they have learned to help others develop into being "more". If you are the superhuman in the room where big decisions are made, then influence what happens in that room for the good. Leverage your access along with your perspective of how everyone brings value to help individuals find as much consensus as possible on optimal solutions.

You don't have to be perfect or know the precise thing to say when you open up and share transparently. Superhumans are not perfect. Sometimes the way we live, or the things we say or do in a particular moment, do not match up to the ambitions we have in our hearts to *be* more and *do* more. But at the end of the day, becoming superhuman is about recognizing that you are a resource to others and that there is no shortage of what you can give to the world from what you have experienced and learned. Recognize that your mistakes, setbacks, and failures are no reason to keep quiet when your words are required or to shrink back when your presence is meaningful. This could mean challenging neighbors and friends in your community to stand up for social justice causes. This could also mean showing up at your local school board meeting and sharing openly about how your professional experience gives you a perspective on ways in which some of the academic programs could be improved. As you share, selflessly, for the greater good, your credibility will grow and you will enable those around you also to grow.

This is how superheroes establish their credibility in comic books and movies—they selflessly give us themselves for the greater good. Even if they initially communicate the wrong message through their approach, they continue to share their gifts with the world until people believe they are for the good, in the face of the bad. In other words, they share the knowledge they have gained through their experiences: that good can prevail in the face of difficult times. By sharing, they build hope and inspire others.

I point to these superhero narrative arcs as a source of inspiration, particularly for those of us who feel as if we got off to a bad start with people, with a job, or in a relationship. Many superhero stories show us how even humans with extraordinary capabilities can get off to a bad start and then neglect to share their gifts with the world. When we look at some of the most influential and accomplished leaders in our world, including political leaders, teachers, doctors, professors, coaches, producers, and public servants, we realize that they want to continue pouring into others, as much as possible.

So, I encourage you to keep sharing the knowledge you have learned from all of your past experiences. You will generate new levels of trust, credibility, and creative confidence in those around you. Develop a "give" mentality, guided by a humble attitude, and share the knowledge you have learned along the way about mindset, relationships, and finances.

As I have gone through the past few years in Silicon Valley, I have made big mistakes, taken huge risks, and even broken hearts with both companies and friends. I have had to apologize, make amends, and learn to be accountable at new levels. I have had to learn how to communicate better and build credibility faster through putting a lot of energy into fast-moving projects and dynamic teams. Sometimes it has worked out great, yet sometimes my performance missed the mark and I had to live with the consequences.

But one thing I have learned that is helping me on my superhuman journey is to design ways to continue sharing information with those around me. I have created messages on different platforms that reveal my journey and expose my weaknesses and strengths. And I have created value by being vulnerable and sharing my story with you. When a blogger requests an interview, I participate. I make margin in my schedule to sit on panels that focus on diversity, inclusion, and belonging. I volunteer with nonprofit organizations that seek to develop young, creative high schoolers in the local community. I even find time to shop at my local farmer's markets and spend my dollars with merchants who make up a viable part of my neighborhood.

There are so many ways to share your knowledge, experience, and expertise. So, stay humble, be honest with yourself, become more vulnerable about your story, and open yourself up as a resource for others. Help those around you learn how to evaluate their lives, become conscious of the world around them, and create better selves for their communities.

Call to Creativity

Actions for Exploring the Superhuman Pillar of Relationships and People

→ Join a local community group focused on positive social missions. This is an environment that fosters the 3 C's of Creativity: consciousness, connection, and community. If done well, these groups can encourage people to be more vulnerable, accountable, and intimate (in a nonsexual way) among a group of individuals all seeking to help each other be better and do more with their lives.

→ Go beyond looking to be inspired by others; become the person who others are inspired by. Practice cultivating an enthusiastic mindset that proactively points to positive outcomes.

→ Social media encourages us to connect with friends, family, and colleagues. Over time, many of us might also gather lots of followers. Don't doubt the power of this extended network; some can be valuable patrons of ideas you want to achieve in the future. Instead, develop this network and build the community by involving them in your dialogue. Help your community feel heard and indispensable. In other words, invest in those who are part of your network by adding value to them; later you will be able to ask for their commitment.

→ Creativity grows with open-minded people. Being open-minded does not mean that you entertain every belief or notion. But it does mean being open to learning about what inspires and even excites other people. Your creative core will grow with colleagues, partners, friends, and community members who are asking questions, seeking to understand different personalities and perspectives, and approaching life with a sense of curiosity.

→ Meaningful relationships are a daily reminder of why we live superhuman-by-design. Though not perfect, our closest relationships are a reminder that we are not living purely for our success and goal-oriented achievement. Instead, we want to multiply the positive experience of others and affect those around us so they can make better decisions and plans in their own lives.

→ Use your superpowers to do for others what they cannot achieve for themselves. As we develop our creativity, the superpowers we bring to the world become more and more evident. A self-centered life that does not see these superpowers as a resource to help others in desperate need will be an unfulfilled life. Remember, superheroes represent the best values of the society they help. So, constantly look for ways your superpowers can make a difference in the lives of others!

SUPERHUMAN RESULTS

The difference between living a life built around material success and a superhuman life comes down to the "why," or the reasons underlying our push for results and the nature of those desired results or achievements. If those achievements are undertaken for reasons beyond our own desires, beyond the good it might do us, then we are truly living superhuman lives. Superhumans recognize that our mission is to achieve goals with as much creativity and character as possible because the impact of that achievement far exceeds the benefits we accrue for ourselves.

Now, before we dive further into the nature of superhuman results and how we know when we are delivering such results, I want to be clear on this point: *there is nothing wrong with being successful.*

I want you to dream big dreams, to accomplish ambitious goals, to live a life filled with success.

In fact, the ability to achieve goals and to commit to a life that requires discipline, energy, and determination is part of what attracts us to superhumans. They leverage their failures as learnings for future successes, and they believe they can outdo themselves each day in their pursuit both of creating more value for others and of being more, as people, for their family, friends, and community.

Such results are not always recognized immediately, and in fact, we do not always see the impact of our own superhuman results initially. But in the end, these are the results that others will remember us for and that they will want to live up to themselves. These are the results that positively impact communities, cities, and countries. Of all our work, these are the results that shape our human existence for the better, enriching our world and becoming iconic moments in the culture at large that give us hope that we can do more than we'd ever thought possible.

Our passion and our creativity not only will bring about the successes we desire in many areas of our lives but also will help to redefine and elevate the world around us.

FROM HERO TO SUPERHERO TO ICON

When writer Jerry Siegel conceived of the superhero character Superman, in the 1930s, he wanted to give him a secret identity that would help him blend in with civilians. Obviously, a guy with a red cape and superhuman strength running around faster than a speeding bullet was not going to "blend in." And so Siegel crafted mild-mannered Clark Kent.

Similarly, Wonder Woman typically disguises herself in the civilian identity of Diana Prince, having left her home island of Themyscira, where she and her fellow Amazonian warriors were hidden from the rest of humanity.

What these and other superhero characters have in common is their initial obscurity. They start off doing what is necessary in order to eventually do what might have once seemed impossible.

In much the same way, our journey to superhuman results is accompanied by initially doing what is necessary.

During my time with startup companies, we would often skip doing what was necessary because we wanted to achieve massive results quickly. I remember being asked to launch marketing campaigns that would overnight attract hundreds of new customers and then watching our unfledged executives dealing with the fallout of not having a customer relationship management tool ready to handle the new business. In the same way, applying the design process to my personal life often required doing the necessary, consistently, over a period of time. For instance, building better relationships with the local community required me to listen to other leaders in the community about the causes they were fighting for. Often I would be required to make room in my schedule in order to be present and to gain credibility with the group. Even when I decided to grow spiritually by taking courses on faith, I had to commit to putting energy into getting to know the elders and pastors. The results early on from these activities sometimes only meant a connection over coffee—but eventually they turned into opportunities with more responsibility and exposure.

The trajectory of becoming superhuman runs parallel to the types of results you are producing to enrich the world around you. In that trajectory, those of us on this journey go from hero to superhero to icon.

Hero

The hero stage is that time in life when you are called on to do the necessary. As someone who is still on the journey, I find that we can all collectively be in some phase of this journey in one of the areas of our lives addressed by the Superhuman Pillars. In these moments, our superpower is situational and we can choose to maximize it for the sake of our own glory or to help others achieve something that seems impossible to them.

One of the things that attracted me most to the startup world was being given the role and responsibility that I wanted before I'd fully proven my capability. It was a risk that matched my desire to prove that I was capable regardless of whether or not I had the experience on paper. My confidence was not connected to my credibility, but rather to my belief in my talent and abilities.

The pitfalls that I thought might come with sudden, superficial success often did not. In other words, when I got the opportunity, I excelled and did not let the job title go to my head. I had the work ethic, the creativity, the intelligence, and I'd even developed enough character to weather some of the prejudice-driven conversations in those big conference room meetings.

But here's what I missed out on through this acceleration: understanding that doing the necessary, though not sexy, is what builds the intangibles that fast, superficial achievements can't produce. It was only after a few years of failures and successes that I began to understand that doing the necessary—or putting in the work over time and building experience—was a way of achieving significantly more in the long run.

What I learned is that doing the necessary gives you the time to grow in knowledge and expertise around the things you want to pursue the most. It also helps you build the stamina to weather the stretches of life when your work or other areas of life seem mundane or challenging. By doing the necessary, I discovered the importance of helping others by serving them. For me, serving others meant helping my family, friends, and colleagues achieve their goals. I learned that doing what is required builds strong muscles of integrity, generosity, and humility. Embracing the requirement of doing what is necessary at the moment helps us learn that true fulfillment will come from enriching others and from helping them achieve things that they never thought possible.

In the hero phases of your superhuman journey, focus on doing what is required in your home, your finances, your health, and your career. You may not realize it, but this consistency is preparing you for not only a future of readily visible success, but also one of deeper though sometimes less tangible success. By being a hero when called on, you act intentionally to enhance the lives of the people you are connected with in your world. In other words, you are becoming superhuman.

So, celebrate the victories—because you will have them!—and honor your wins and accomplishments. Just realize that as these applause-worthy moments come farther and farther apart, you'll be entering another phase on your journey.

Superhero

Once you have begun doing what's necessary and experiencing the personal highs of success for doing what you have been asked to do, you'll be given more authority and responsibility. In my experience, this phase comes when people see the *value* you have been creating by delivering on the necessary. You will also sense that you are entering this phase because now, more than ever, you will have a deepening desire to engage in doing more so as to help larger audiences, communities, and groups experience life-changing results and see the impact of those results in shared environments.

Welcome to the superhero phase.

This phase is about not only doing what is required but also beginning to think about how to do what is possible for yourself and for others. Superheroes are those of us on the superhuman journey who have developed a positive outlook and who seek to solve difficult problems to make things better for many.

At this stage, I have learned that exercising the Superhuman Code in your character is more important than ever because others are depending on your superhuman results. Again, think about what makes a hero a superhero: it is not just the fact that they have extraordinary powers, which they employ to do what is required of them (for example, stopping a plane full of passengers from crashing), but also that they've been recognized in the community as having a high degree of integrity. They have achieved this by delivering superhuman results that fulfill the commitments they've made to be greater not for personal gain, but to help others.

This can be a tiring role to fulfill, and that's why engaging in activities that promote your most creative self is so important. Often in this phase, you are pushing a group to higher levels of performance—whether it be your children in their academic growth or a team at work. You are creating a culture and honoring that culture by constantly aligning what you say and what you do. Remaining limber and creative enables you to bring your best to the task every day.

For me, the most exciting superhero phase of my journey was building Forecast Studios to be a sought-after creative agency. My ethical obligation to the creative team that had been with me at Skully, along with my motivation to help our entire group succeed, aligned with my ability to pitch and win business. This led to a number of significant financial and social gains for our team and eventually put us in rooms with CEOs and Chief Marketing Officers who saw the value we had created for other companies in the Bay Area. Through our success, we rebuilt our careers after the bankruptcy of Skully, and so we were able to continue living gainfully in the most expensive city in the US.

Beyond the increases in authority, responsibility, and influence, this phase is characterized by what people share with you. I am not just talking about the proverbial pat on the back, but about the thoughtful and appreciative comments recognizing the value of your work. Those are powerful moments in the superhuman life. In those moments, you'll have tangible evidence that you're making a difference. You're wearing the cape!

Icon

As we journey further into our lives, living as much as possible with the intent of both working harder and being more, for ourselves and others, we enter into the final phase of a superhuman life, the icon stage. I have not reached this stage in my superhuman journey, but I marvel at others who have and who are living the icon journey into their late years.

It is in this stage that a superhuman transcends the expectations of others, transcends doing what is possible, and begins accomplishing the seemingly impossible. The contributions of this superhuman have become so noteworthy that they now command great respect and admiration. These are the superhumans who have dedicated their lives to positively affecting the world and enriching the lives of many.

There are many such icons. These men and women are the superhumans we recognize in our literature, our foundations, and even our holidays.

Sometimes the superhumans who affect our lives the most are the ones who knew it the least. In my case, my grandfather, Johnny B. Harris, was such a superhuman.

When my grandfather passed in 2011, it was a cold and snowy day in Atlanta. It usually does not snow in Atlanta, so when it does, the entire city seems to shut down. I was at a cafe connected to my apartment when I got the call. Of course, losing a close family member is always hard, but losing my grandfather felt different. It felt like a gap had opened up in my life, as if every time I saw a picture of him, he had been cut out and there was now nothingness, a blank.

He'd made such an impression on me, had been so important in my life, and I realized that most sharply, now that he was gone.

My grandfather was of a generation that I could never fully understand. He had fought wars in foreign lands, all with the deep, gut-sickening awareness that his mere existence as a Black man in America was fraught with danger. Here, in his own country, he was often thought of as other, as intruder, as barely a second-class citizen. He was hated not for who he was, but for who others thought he was. And he could pay for that perception with his health, or with his life, at any time, on any day.

This was the generation of Black Americans who had made the great journey away from the sharecropping South to the growing industrial metropolises of the North during the early 1920s. This was also the generation who knew from hard experience the tragedy and violence of racism, who'd lived under a legal system that regarded Black Americans as less than full citizens, as less than full persons. It was a time when a day's work meant long, long hours filled with achingly physical labor.

My grandfather worked hard all of his life. As a young man, he became a colonel in the US Army and enlisted during the Korean War. After the army, he landed a job at the Ford Motor Company in Chicago, where he worked until he retired thirty years later. Throughout his time with the company, my grandfather made friends and built relationships with his coworkers that would last the rest of his life. He also started a candy business that netted him cash every day.

As a kid, I called him the "Candy Papa" because he would always have candy or cash for me whenever I saw him. He stood just over six foot two, with broad shoulders and big, gnarled hands, so it was always fun to see him lean down and open up a palm full of peppermints or five-dollar bills.

Johnny B. was a man of few words, but his actions left a great impression on me. He did not know much about investing, but he created generational wealth for my entire family by purchasing properties. At some point, he bought a three-story apartment building on the South Side of Chicago and restored it. He rented out the apartments and used the additional income to purchase other properties back in his home state of Missouri. All the while, he managed to raise four children and to get them safely through high school during some of the most radical and political days in the city.

With me, my grandfather also was a man of action. He was always showing me something, not just telling me something. He would show me how to bait a hook and fish for catfish, how to work on a car, or how he managed the inventory of candy he sold at work. All of his actions seemed to make the lives of others better—not just his immediate family, but his extended family, his friends, and ultimately the neighbors he lived beside for much of his life. He never seemed to be a man who sought recognition, but he was quick to recognize the hard work and diligence of those around him, including me.

I credit him with inspiring me to live a life beyond mediocrity, for striving to do more than just what is asked of me. I credit him also with being an inspiration to *do* more and to *be* more for others.

Though he did not retire with millions, he finished his last years fulfilled and full of generosity, love, and life experience. He was a superhuman, a person of reverence for many and a model for even more. At the funeral, when the pastor addressed the large gathering, asking who represented my grandfather, in one poetic moment, fifteen older men in suits stood up to recognize him. All of them were lifelong friends and colleagues from the Ford Motor Company. All of them had shown up to pay their respects to Johnny B.

MAKING HEADLINES

How do we know that we've achieved a truly superhuman result? How do we know that we've done something more than simply reaching our goal, something more than experiencing a moment of success?

Ask yourself: did I change the outcome?

You see, superhuman results are about more than awakening your inner superperson. Even more, such results are not about being recognized by others or giving yourself a self-congratulatory parade. Superhuman results are about how you influenced the outcome. As superhumans we are excited about the outcomes we achieve as well as the new possibilities that open up. These results will be different for everyone, but one thing they'll have in common is that the outcomes are driven in part by you.

When this starts to happen, when what you do affects the outcome, you'll start to make headlines. And there's another clue that you're on the right track.

What are headlines? Let's take a look again at our superhero friends.

The classic comic books were filled with expressive and bold visuals.

The cover pages were arresting to the eye. Inside, advertisements for toys and other comic books would burst through the main story lines. Within the stories themselves, the reigning superhero often made the front page of the city's newspaper with some daring feat that saved the day. We can all relate to those superhero headlines roaring off the press to let the world know that someone has done something great that made a difference. The headlined story would also be a reminder for the populace of the tragedy, disaster, or menace that could have led to lives lost if it were not for the swift and positive action of this superhero.

You'll know that you are achieving superhuman results when others begin to talk about how you're bringing change, about how you're improving outcomes in a big way. As superhumans, this is not our motivation, but it is critical to understand that making headlines is an important indicator of having a positive effect on the lives of others. It is also critical to understand that at any given point, we might be making headlines in some areas but not others. That's all part of it. As imperfect humans, we are subject to falling short as we commit to new superhuman tasks. Building consistency takes time, and opening ourselves up creatively requires opening up maybe more than we are comfortable with at any given moment.

But in the end, it's worth it. Whether it's one person—a student, perhaps, inspired by a teacher to achieve more—or many, as with a minister who grows her ministry to positively influence the way people serve and meet the needs of others in the community, changing outcomes is what gets superhumans out of bed every day.

As the world rolls on, I have learned that the time in between headlines is no reflection of whether or not I am excited about chasing my potential. The headlines are only the indicators that some of your work has been recognized. They do not lay out the creative process you've engaged in to build your creative core and generate stunning results. This is why it is so important not to stop when you receive praise from people. While praise provides temporary validation, we as superhumans are motivated by chasing our greater purpose to *do* more and to *be* more.

I am right here with you on the path of desiring to make superhuman results come to life. Every day, I am exploring the full range of my creative capacities to design a life that yields superhuman results. The encouragement I give myself, and that I would also give you, is to unleash your most creative self into the world every day and know that the results will come. It is extremely rare for superhumans to remain in obscurity. We are too bright to hide, and our deep desire to become synonymous with impact is too strong.

Don't let self-doubt and insecurity stop you from trying to climb this hill. Your peak performance is not capped by anything but you—so commit to living superhuman-by-design in order to produce superhuman results!

GETTING
T

PART THREE

GETTING STARTED: TAKEOFF

LIFESAVERS

As you prepare to begin your journey, it's time to think again about that all-important aspect of our lives: community. And with community, connection.

By this point, you've spent a lot of time thinking about how you'll begin living the superhuman life, about what you'll do, whom you'll help, and what you'll accomplish. But in the very beginning, and occasionally too when you hit roadblocks along the way, it's worth thinking about who can help you.

Just as you while living your superhuman life will be working to help others, eventually even becoming an inspirational model for this approach to life, there are others out there now, living strong in the superhuman life, who can help *you*. Nowhere does this come so perfectly into play, perhaps, than when you are just starting out.

Such superhumans act as lifesavers, and they can help us enormously.

TWO KEY WAYS THAT LIFESAVERS HELP US

Of the many ways that other superhumans can help us, two in particular stand out, both having to do with helping to prepare us against fear. The fears—of what might go wrong and the fear that can sometimes follow when something *has* gone wrong.

Fear itself is inevitable. It's woven into the fabric of our subconscious. Entrepreneurs, artists, evangelists, teachers, and leaders in every generation have understood that some of the greatest difficulties in living beyond the average involve facing our fears. That's why in the narrative of the superhero we so often find the theme of conquering fear.

It is this facing and overcoming of fear that we find particularly inspiring—because we have all experienced how when we allow our fears to paralyze us, we cannot move forward. The most prominent superhumans, past and present, acknowledge that without facing our fears, we will not be able to make any significant and dramatic changes in our lives. In other words, there's a connection between fear and failure, a point they often address as well. Former US First Lady Michelle Obama, who speaks on topics ranging from education to racial injustice, and whose work on humanitarian issues has inspired men and women across the world, has this to say about the danger of succumbing to fear:

> ***Failure is a feeling long before it becomes an actual result. It's vulnerability that breeds with self-doubt and then is escalated, often deliberately, by fear.***

As a creative, I am always facing some new problem or challenge that requires an innovative spirit. The blank page or the clean canvas is still simultaneously one of the most exhilarating and one of the most alarming things for me. To this day, giving a presentation in front of an audience of peers or a roomful of executives gets my palms sweating and my heart racing. Even having difficult conversations with neighbors or family members can be intimidating. When we commit to conquering fears related to our goals, we must first acknowledge those fears, and then face them by pushing forward in our commitment to better ourselves—despite the difficulty. By lingering in thoughts about what might happen, we risk the consequence of never getting started on the journey.

Fear such as this can prevent us from starting. But there is also the fear that follows a mistake or misstep. We all know that sinking feeling when something goes wrong. And in fact, when something goes terribly wrong, we might wish for an Undo key. But there is no such escape hatch. Instead, we'll need to live with those mistakes. The encouraging news is that there are many people living superhuman lives right now who have also made mistakes along the way. I certainly am one of them!

Mistakes need not deter us from our path.

The best way to deal with mistakes, of course, is to learn from them, so that we make the mistakes part of the journey. So that we're always improving. The superhuman path calls for that and more. It invites us to look more deeply into the lives of other people living their purpose, full of intention, courage, and confidence, and to learn from them. It calls for us to invite such superhumans into our lives as lifesavers.

Learning from such lifesavers reinforces the power of connection and community, two of the 3 C's of Creativity. Instead of looking with dismay at the rubble of the mistakes we've made, we can turn our attention to those who continue to focus on bringing value to the world, despite any errors on their part. We can do the same. Mistakes are all part of the process.

And when we allow lifesavers in, to help energize and motivate our own journey—and to help us over the inevitable hurdles later on—we are inviting in the same help that we will one day turn around and offer others.

BUILDING YOUR INNER CIRCLE

It's clear that we need lifesavers in our lives. But here's the thing: you can't count on them just showing up. True enough, as a person of faith and someone who has sought to live a Christian life, I believe that God can create "divine appointments," life-changing interactions with people we would have never expected to meet.

Regardless, we must also actively work toward making the right things happen. We cannot be passive, expecting divine intervention to rescue us. It is up to us to seek out positive and life-affirming people. To choose the friends, mentors, and coaches who can hold us accountable in accomplishing our dreams and goals, and who can inspire and encourage us to do so. To choose to associate with those who are themselves striving to achieve more with their lives, rather than with toxic individuals who can feed our minds with doubt and fear and who can turn us away from the higher journey in any number of ways. Some of the biggest deterrents, when we first start out on the journey to becoming superhuman, can come from our inner circles. The path to becoming superhuman takes time, consistency, and association with both the dreamers and the doers in your world. That's why the relationships pillar is so important. Without strong, deep relationships with a circle of people who want you to accomplish more, you will quickly fade back to an average life.

Oh, sure, there are the isolated cases of sudden success. But these are not the sorts of success that anyone can predict or build on. Winning a lottery, for example, can make for an amazing day, but that windfall of riches does not prepare an individual for the headwinds ahead. To design a better life for ourselves and those we love takes dedication and effort.

OK, let's take a step back and lighten the mood.

When I was young, one of my very favorite things to do was to wake up early on Saturday morning for cartoons. This was in Dallas, before we moved to the Midwest. In summer, it was often too hot during the first half of the day to go outside and play. And honestly, I did not want to go outside because there were cartoon options galore for me to chase from channel to channel. My two favorites at the time were the Ninja Turtles and the Justice League animated series. The tapestry of superhero narratives and colorful outfits was a dream. Every episode seemed to find a way to bring all of the characters onto the scene together to face some seemingly impossible crisis. So, of course, I was delighted as an adult to see how DC introduced the Justice League to the big screen.

No matter the battle, members of the Justice League found a way to leverage each other's powers to defeat the enemy. More often than not, this meant squashing their egos and humbling themselves enough to understand that their superpowers alone were not sufficient to accomplish every mission and win every battle.

While it might feel like a stretch to relate this to our own circumstances and realities, the inner circles we are a part of make a huge difference in our superhuman journey. Becoming superhuman-by-design is not about success alone. Developing an inner circle that is positive and supportive does not guarantee success. But it will help you do something that is difficult for everyone on this journey: not give up.

You can't go it alone. Surround yourself with good people. Surround yourself with support.

Building Your "Circle of Inspiration"

The personal relationships that we develop are crucial for the journey, but it is not just in these relationships that we can turn to lifesavers. Potential lifesavers are all around us in the world. We buy their books at the airport before a long flight. We stream their podcasts while taking long walks. We attend their conferences. And we even pay hundreds, sometimes thousands, of dollars to sit with them in smaller groups to learn how they were able to achieve such heights despite adversity.

When we invite these larger-than-life superhumans into our lives, to listen to them and to learn from them, drawing from their wisdom and strength, we are building for ourselves a "circle of inspiration." Though we do not have the daily personal interaction with such lifesavers that we have with people in our inner circle, they can nonetheless be a significant force in our lives.

As you prepare for the journey, look to your personal life and look also outside your own circle, to the superhumans out in the world who are accessible through either the knowledge they share or the presence they invite you to experience. These too could be your lifesavers, providing you with inspiration and initiative, motivation, and models for undertaking the journey successfully.

LAUNCHPAD

So now you know about the importance of the creative core and how to nurture it. You know how to explore thoughts, concepts, and tasks by applying the design process. You know about the foundational superpowers and how to develop your own. You know about the Superhuman Code and the Superhuman Pillars. And you know about lifesavers.

But where should you begin? How do you actually get started? Here are a few principles to help you with those first steps.

THINK: CONSIDER YOUR VOICES

Whom we listen to and how we talk to ourselves can determine the steadiness of our journey—and how long it takes us to get started down the path.

How often have you replayed in your mind something someone said to you earlier that day, that week? Someone asking you to consider a different point of view or to reconsider a decision. Someone making a great point that perhaps you were too busy, or too stubborn, to listen to earlier. And of course, you think also about what *you* said, or ought to have said, in return.

Our thoughts represent the conversations we are constantly having with ourselves. During quiet moments, when we are alone and undistracted, we can better hear the things we are saying to ourselves—and the things that others have said that we are replaying in our minds .

Our minds are the servants of our thoughts. Those thoughts can paralyze us, or they can free us to take charge and act. And those thoughts are shaped by the many voices we hear around us. The voices of family, friends, colleagues, influencers, the media—whatever and whomever we listen to. Before we internalize those beliefs about the world and about ourselves, we feed them with the voices we listen to.

When I decided to become a Christian, I thought that my moments with God would become audible. As if I would actually hear a booming voice or a sweet whisper. But what I found was that the clearest God-like thoughts often came through the conversations in my mind as I was praying or meditating on a scripture.

So, why is the topic of voices so critical to launching into the journey of becoming superhuman-by-design? Because our inner voice is powerful. It can urge us on, or it can hold us back.

If you take control, shaping your thoughts to support the journey, you will have greater success. When I review my own journey, I see that a key factor between living unstructured and living connected to the superhuman journey has been my inner voice. And when your focus is on driving toward becoming superhuman-by-design, your inner voice can help better connect you to that greater purpose.

Take the example of retired Navy Seal David Goggins, author of *Can't Hurt Me: Master Your Mind and Defy the Odd*s. In his book, Goggins shares ways to strengthen the mind so as to be able to take on whatever life serves up. But one lesson in particular focuses squarely on the power of our inner voices and why it is so critical to become aware of these voices as we strive to change and improve. Goggins writes that we all have two inner voices: one is trying to direct us to a place where we can be better, and the other is one of comfort, tempting us to take the path of least resistance. How can we experience any transformational gains and become better unless we harden ourselves against the voices of comfort?

In the world of superheroes, too, those doers of good must sometimes overcome their own inner voices of doubt, indecision, and fear. One of the newer entries into the pantheon, Disney/Pixar's *The Incredibles*, plays adroitly on this division of purpose and lack of confidence that we in the movie audience know all too well. As the story unfolds, we often hear the inner thoughts of the characters, and so we are privy to their doubts and fears. What I find exciting about the construct of the film is that taking charge of our inner voice is not only about hurtling past the really challenging moments of life and being tough. It's also about taking control so that we can navigate toward a life filled with purpose and meaning.

So, how do we develop the inner dialogue that enables us to rise above difficult moments, that encourages us to be "more"? How do we design a superhuman mind with an inner voice that lifts us to new heights? By exercising a principle I call the "voice of vision." Developing your voice of vision is like learning a new language. And it is work that you'll need to undertake every day.

Some of the most beautiful things we enjoy in the world today come from the people who have harnessed their doubt and instead connected with their vision. Designers, artists, composers, poets, philosophers—all have had to develop and then listen to their voices of vision. When we begin speaking to ourselves with the voice of vision, we can start our path toward designing confident and influential lives, no matter our circumstances.

I have found that the most successful people in my life pay attention to their inner voice and to the stories they tell themselves. They have often pointed out how the voices of others can influence our own voice and beliefs. I have personally found that when I have the wrong voices around me, my own voice becomes stifled both outwardly and inwardly. I have also found that by speaking to myself about my dreams and deepest personal revelations, I have gained greater mental clarity about the steps to take to move toward my purpose on that day. For me, the podcast *Affirmation Pod* has been a valuable resource as I learn to examine my thoughts.

It is up to you to decide how you want to work through the design process to hone the most uplifting and supportive inner voice. In my process, I research informative and empowering messages. As I summarize my findings from the insights of other superhumans, I write out specific aspects of my life where I want to see change. Absorbing these messages fuels my mind with thoughts that keep me open to new resources and creative about how to navigate toward my goals. I hope that as you ideate, prototype, and test which materials inspire the most imaginative and optimistic voice of vision in yourself, you return also to this book.

FEEL: PURSUE CREATIVE GENEROSITY

Millennials, as a generation, are typically portrayed as self-centered and boldly pursuing the easiest paths to happiness. In fact, many studies, including one in 2017 from *Forbes*, show that millennials think that success in life is more about happiness than material prosperity.

Of course, we all want happiness. But we're not always sure how to define it. My time in Silicon Valley has been punctuated by periods in which I pursued happiness doggedly through to professional success. Yet when success came, along with material gain, I often felt disconnected from the project, even discontented.

The burnouts, those stretches of extreme exhaustion, were often followed by binges in spending or chasing the "good life" through parties and invite-only events. I found myself in a cycle that would lift and then sink me like an old-fashioned roller coaster on a boardwalk. I started to call this cycle the *happiness loop*. This is the cycle that kicks in when we focus primarily on what makes us feel good. Instead of test driving, or prototyping, new ways of engaging the world around us with our superpowers, we use those powers primarily for our own short-lived enjoyment. Quite often, as I have seen in my own life, this produces a life focused on materialism, but hollow in meaning.

When I first recognized this, it was a crucial lesson. New to the superhuman journey, I had learned the importance of creating value *for* others, but I had not applied my superpowers to actually helping others.

I started exploring how to *do* more and *be* more through the design process. I had been practicing strengthening the Superhuman Pillars, so my creative core was strong. I knew how to engage with ideas, how to get them to flow freely. To quiet my mind and purge myself of fear-driven thoughts, I began to practice meditation more deeply. My spiritual life became stronger as I carved out more space in my life for prayer. I began simplifying my physical surroundings, creating rooms that were cleaner and more spare. For a time, I dedicated weekends to serving at a homeless shelter in downtown San Francisco. All of these activities helped me turn more of my focus to others and their needs. It had become evident to me that superhumans design not only ways to create value for those around them, but also ways to serve those people.

As I continued to prototype ways to give, I discovered that the most fulfilling way of creating value and also serving others was to offer something that people desperately needed and could not afford, but that I could create. It gives me great joy to create visual elements like logos, brand guidelines, and websites for new churches and nonprofits, or for local businesses looking to serve their community. Meaningful, too, has been working with kids to help them prepare for a career in design.

So, no matter what you try out in your path as a superhuman, I encourage you to simply start. Whom do you empathize with in your world? Whom can you create value for, and who needs your help the most? By finding the intersections between the issues that matter the most to you and the things you can do to help others, you can find ways to be creatively generous to the world. Local, regional, and global organizations need superhumans who can look beyond themselves to bring their time, talents, and energy to the table.

As superhumans, we escape the ephemeral and fickle happiness loop that comes with chasing only our own material success and accomplishments, finding deeper meaning and satisfaction by instead giving of ourselves to the world.

PRACTICE: DEVELOP YOUR HABITS AND RITUALS

Developing strong habits is going to be important, right from the start. In fact, developing those strong habits will help you get started.

One of my earliest memories as a child was of discovering how to apply my mind to a task in order to be more efficient. Whatever the task, if I could figure out a smoother and more ingenious way to accomplish it, I was immediately attracted to that approach.

Perhaps this was just the way my mind worked at the time. I was fascinated by a process that yielded the same result, often a reward, but with greater efficiency. Discovering that I was able to remember these streamlined processes and with practice to then convert them into habits gave me those first insights into how our behaviors are shaped by daily decisions. It taught me that the pathways of our brain can be trained. As I grew older, I recognized that I operated very well off triggers, or cues, that would prompt the rest of the behavior, running it like a script.

To a degree, we all operate off cues. As we saw in the superpowers chapter, we can use visual cues as tangible anchors to trigger our minds to refocus on the task at hand. Our brains work hard to make almost any action we do daily into a programmable algorithm, primed to look for efficiencies to achieve the same results. The enlightening discovery for me was the realization that by anchoring what I did in consciousness, the first of the 3 C's of Creativity, I could create habits that support becoming superhuman-by-design, rather than creating habits haphazardly.

Our worst habits—the ones we most regret—are often encoded unconsciously. One of my favorite reads on habits comes from James Clear, who says that habits are often formed as "the result of many small choices made over time," without our even realizing it. In my experience, these tend to be the habits that are etched into my system by my taking the path of least resistance.

As people on the path to being superhuman, we have to consciously create habits in our lives that purposefully drive us toward our highest potential. To live superhuman-by-design, we have to put in the daily effort to develop practices that strengthen our resolve and grow our character.

Without examining how the right and wrong habits form in our lives, we lose the ability to see how small beneficial behaviors over time lead to big results. We lose touch with our design process.

The habits introduced in this book are designed to help you become more conscious of the world around you, of your biases, and of your deep and creative self. I can tell you that cultivating a habit of writing every day is the only reason this book came to life. But writing a book was only a part of the vision. Ultimately, striving to live superhuman-by-design was about establishing new rhythms in my life that would inspire me to give more to others around me through my craft.

STRATEGIZE: WORK THE FOUR CORNERS, THEN GO OUTSIDE THE BOX

When you begin ideating, then when you move to prototyping, it's important to realize that you needn't "reinvent the wheel." You don't have to generate a groundbreaking, never-seen-before idea to successfully accomplish a dream or goal. When it comes to becoming superhuman in our everyday lives, we must design strategies that help us think innovatively, but we should not be dismissive of trusted and proven processes.

Early in my career as a designer, I struggled with this concept. Later, I discovered that this is a common misconception among many creative, entrepreneurially minded professionals early in their careers. In Silicon Valley, where the push is particularly to come up with completely new processes and "disruptive" measures, this misconception can be pervasive.

In 2019 author and entrepreneur Virginia Heffernan wrote an article for *Wired* describing the mindset of tech startups that used marketing to disguise the gaps in their products, putting market success above all else. She writes:

> ***Four years ago, when companies had profound problems with their models, leadership, or products, marketing came to be seen as not just a way to lipstick pigs but as a way to block and tackle regulation, to keep secrets, to shut out anyone who wanted to so much as see the product.***

As a participant in a company that relied heavily on marketing tactics to camouflage its internal issues, I understand the temptation to skip critical aspects of business development so as to have quick market success. In some instances, I watched as leaders spoke persuasively about how they could assemble a team of talented individuals to solve problems on the fly. The volatile startup environments that I walked through seemed to always be on the knife-edge of either steep success or plunging failure. The tension was palpable, but management teams often could not be convinced to travel the tried and true when developing their product strategies.

During this period in the Valley, the idea of working on a tight budget to develop a fantastic product would often give way to figuring out ways to create dynamic, sexy presentations that would elicit greater and greater investments from venture capitalists. The established methods for developing tight-knit contracts, assembling and nurturing all-star teams, and creating civil and socially inclusive environments were dismissed in the mistaken idea that accomplishing something groundbreaking must also require throwing out anything and everything reminiscent of the old guard.

Bottom line: there is something to be said for adopting a strategy that has been proven, repeatedly, by other successful individuals. This does not diminish the fact that you may also develop a completely new way to accomplish a goal or a dream. Whatever you do will indeed be unique to you. However, there is considerable value in first trying things that are already working. I have found this to be true, time and again, both at the office and in my personal life.

For instance, there are professionals out there who have struggled with some of the same fears you face and yet have managed to accomplish much more than the average. What did they do? How did they do it? With all of the resources of the web now at our fingertips, we can research their stories, and if they write, we can also seek out their own reflections for deeper insights. We can adopt some of their strategies and make those strategies our own. Whether it is raising kids or entertaining a career pivot, looking to others first can provide you with viable strategies to try. Homing in on the leadership of others so as to help spur our own growth is, again, taking into consideration the relationships pillar.

I call this method "working the four corners." We're not yet "outside the box." We're first making better use of the resources available to us *inside* the box. In this, I am not advocating that we simply follow someone else's path to achieving a superhuman life. But we *can* take steps to design aspects of our process in light of what other successful individuals have done in the past. Before I "go outside the box" and scout around for a new process, I think through the different approaches and perspectives that have worked for others.

How do I do this? By asking myself lots of questions as I think through my process to *doing* more and *being* more in my own life. For example, am I approaching other professionals to get their opinions? Or am I just hanging out with amateurs who make excuses about why they are not taking the next step? Am I reading material that is helping my mindset in a specific area of my life? Or am I absorbing lots of media that is distracting me from my goals? Am I learning how other superhumans went from A to B and even getting their input? Or am I spending time trusting my own strategy to accomplish a goal?

I encourage you to get honest with yourself. Are you tapping into the resources around you and leveraging strategies that have helped others live what you would consider a superhuman life? Are you building the type of self-awareness that keeps you humble and open to hearing about—and learning from—the successful strategies of those you admire before applying your own spin?

If so, you're ready. You've completed your preparation. It's time.

THREE, TWO, ONE... LAUNCH

You now have a new way of embracing the challenges of life, indeed of creating a life. Should you so choose it.

By strengthening your creative core and approaching both the things you *must* do and the things you would *like* to do with the design process in mind, you will experience an exhilarating new sense of purpose, satisfaction, and meaning. The changes you are making will begin to inspire others, which will likely lead to working more closely with family, friends, and work colleagues in a whole range of new ways. Listen to your clear inner voice. Pay attention to those who believe in you. Be creatively generous. Be mindful of the habits you are cultivating. Don't reinvent what doesn't need reinventing. And no matter what you face as you prepare to launch into the journey, know that you are incredibly special and that so many people need you to lean into your potential. In fact, they are counting on it.

So, go ahead—be superhuman-by-design and change our world for the better!

THE STORY

EPILOGUE

What is it about the end of a thing that brings us back to the beginning? It could be a relationship, a relocation, a job, or a project of some sort—anything new we've embarked on. When we come to the end of it, we may find ourselves looking back to the beginning of the journey.

Sometimes we imagine what could have made it better, what we might have done differently. Perhaps we wonder why we first chose the particular path we took, or about who or what influenced us.

Now that I'm nearing the end of this project, I find myself thinking back to that moment in 2018 when I found myself in a lull, my confidence and energy flagging. I was wondering whether I could make it my daily practice to strive toward the superhuman life that I envisioned. And then a story—the right story at the right moment—turned everything around.

Here's how that happened. Here's the story of that story.

When I transitioned from San Francisco to Marin County, I was in search of a new environment that would allow me to recover and grow from a period of personal disappointment in my life. In Mill Valley, I soon realized the health benefits, mentally and physically, of hiking the scenic coastal trails. One of my favorite hikes was the Tennessee Valley Trail, a relatively easy three-mile hike with a smooth descent that ended on a secluded beach with breathtaking views of the Pacific Ocean.

I often hiked this trail on Sundays. Walking this vast and open space became a way of processing my thoughts at the end of a long week and preparing for the week to come. It was on such a Sunday that I came face to face with the power of self-revelation through a startling encounter with another person on the trail.

I'd decided to stop and sketch for a few minutes, losing myself on a page, when suddenly I was interrupted by a raspy voice with a noticeably Australian accent. I looked up and saw a woman who was perhaps in her early forties, though it was difficult to determine her age because she was in such impeccable shape. Her abs glistened in the afternoon sunshine and she had the bubbly energy of a runner who'd only paused her sprint momentarily because she'd caught sight of my pad.

She noticed that I was sketching shoes and immediately launched into a series of questions to determine whether I was indeed a shoe designer. I could not believe my luck because later that week I would be presenting athletic shoe designs to a potential client. Turns out that not only was I speaking with someone who was an expert on running shoes, but I had actually met a professional marathoner! She was and is a ranked marathoner in Australia, and she had won the Nike Women's Marathon in 2012.

Later, when I researched her, the list of accolades and accomplishments stretched beyond my browser page. But it wasn't her notoriety or fame that stayed with me. It was her ability to pierce my own personal fog regarding how to begin the process of becoming superhuman. I knew why I wanted to be superhuman, and I knew that I wanted this for others. But the sheer weight associated with the task of becoming superhuman in my own life felt overwhelming. In those few minutes, this marathoner did something that I had not been able to do on my own: *she helped me launch*. She shared with me the insight that on a trail, a mind that's resolute is the most powerful factor for determining whether, and how, someone finishes the race. As for progress along the way, it wasn't the entire race a runner was to be thinking of, but just the one moment. One moment at a time.

Sitting in her shadow and listening to her insights on running, I suddenly realized that the path to being superhuman was not something that required me to refocus my entire life all at once. I also realized that I did not have to produce a step-by-step guide for others to follow. Instead, just as the marathoner steps onto the trail each day with a resolute mind, determined to complete her daily miles, I needed to make up my mind to invest in one area to change—one area where spectacular results would inspire me to continue working on other areas of my life—and to do the daily work. One area, or pillar, at a time. One day at a time. Using the 3 C's to nurture my creative core. Harnessing the design process to work on the foundational superpowers and any extensions to those foundations that I would explore. Breaking code to guide focus and energy and to remind me of the deeper purpose of my journey.

I found my way that day on the trail. I hope that with this book I have helped you to find yours.

ACKNOWLEDGMENTS

First and foremost, I need to thank the Ultimate Creator, who has designed so many ways for us, His creation, to bring all goodness and beauty into even the darkest corners of humanity. I am thankful that God gave us the Message, His Word, to help us walk through this side of eternity. As I have journeyed through the past several years, I recognize that it is my faith in His son, Jesus Christ, that has allowed me to make sense of the world.

A special recognition to my developmental editor and book architect, Odile Sullivan-Tarazi, who believed in the power of the material for *Superhuman-by-Design*. Through transparent and deep collaboration, Odile became the first editor to really help craft the original manuscript and bring the best out in me as a new author.

Finally, I would like to thank my parents, Donald Burlock, Sr., and Shelia Burlock, for the incredible sacrifices they have made over the years to give me and my siblings, Melissa and Sylvia, a hope and a future. Their lives have been an example to us of believing in more and living for a purpose higher than our own self-fulfillment. It is a blessing to have a loving family and parents who encourage me to pursue my wildest dreams.

NOTES

Epigraphs

If you make yourself more than just a man: *Batman Begins* (2005). *Batman Begins* is a film directed by Christopher Nolan, starring Christian Bale, Michael Cain, Liam Neeson, and Katie Holmes. The movie shows the transformation of Bruce Wayne into Batman. After training with his mentor, Wayne returns to Gotham and under the superhero identity of Batman begins to rid the city of crime and corruption.

While many superheroes come by their superpowers: McKay and McKay (2011). This quote is from an article in *The Art of Manliness*, an online magazine created by Brett and Kate McKay. Though the site and its accompanying podcast are advertised to a masculine audience, the no-fluff, actionable content is meant for any reader hoping to become better in all areas of their life.

Prologue

xxi **has this to say about the power of story**: Heath and Heath (2008), p. 206. This book by Chip and Dan Heath is a bestseller inspired by Malcolm Gladwell's *The Tipping Point* (2000). The book focuses on storytelling and provides insights on how to craft a compelling narrative. The authors refer to the concept of "stickiness," which was introduced in Gladwell's book and addresses the psychology behind why some ideas are unforgettable. The Heath brothers illustrate these principles through a host of stories and examples.

Introduction

3 **The butterfly effect**: For a clear and concise discussion of this phenomenon and how it is often misconstrued, see Vernon (2017).

5 **Ken Jeong**: Jeong was a practicing physician before landing his first major screen role, playing a doctor in the 2007 movie *Knocked Up*. He went on to a big break role in the wildly popular 2009 movie *The Hangover*, in which he plays the infamous drug-lord villain Mr. Chow. Jeong had always had an interest in drama, but in college decided to pursue a medical career first because he was already a pre-med major. He continued to explore his creativity and eventually became successful in Hollywood.

Chapter 1

8 **For Campbell, a hero is someone**: Campbell (1991), p. 151. This quote originally comes from Campbell's discussions with Bill Moyers in *Joseph Campbell and The Power of Myth* (1988), a six-part PBS television series on the influence of myth on both literature and our lives.

8 **and build on it further**: Rosenberg and Coogan (2013), p. 1.

8 **says that they share**: Fingeroth (2004), p. 17.

9 **$2 billion in worldwide grosses**: Mendelson (2019).

10 **their most distinguishing feature**: Rosenberg (2013), p. 17.

14 **designing by doing**: Brown (2009), p. 124.

15 **IDEO partner Tom Kelley**: Kelley and Littman (2001), p. 13.

Chapter 2

21 **John C. Maxwell**: Maxwell (2010), p. 9.

22 **One scientist and viral immunologist**: For more on Dr. Corbett and the work being undertaken at the Vaccine Research Center, check out the May 21, 2020, episode of the podcast *Speaking of Science* (https://irp.nih.gov/podcast/2020/05/dr-kizzmekia-corbett-the-novel-coronavirus-vaccine).

24 **She puts it this way**: As quoted in Smith (2019).

Chapter 3

39 **A fellow designer recommended a book**: Glei (2013).

Chapter 4

47 **The authors make the point that**: Crowe and McDowell (2017).

48 **Kazuo Inamori**: As cited on his website, at https://global.kyocera.com/inamori/philosophy/philosophy23.html.

53 **a detailed description of ego archetypes**: Black and Hughes (2017).

59 **Simon Sinek**: An inspiring read from author and motivational speaker Sinek, *Start with Why: How Great Leaders Inspire Everyone to Take Action* (2009) is a guide to discovering what makes you feel passionate about your goal. For his 2017 book *Find Your Why: A Practical Guide for Discovering Purpose for You and Your Team*, Sinek partnered with David Mead and Peter Docker to expand beyond the discovery of individual purpose to also finding it for your team or organization.

60 **Sun Tzu**: Written around the fifth century BCE, Sun Tzu's *The Art of War* is a treatise primarily focused on aspects of warfare and how those principles apply to military strategy and tactics. Many authors have since revisited *The Art of War* to write about practical life lessons and business strategies gleaned from the work.

Chapter 6

94 **There is a verse in the Bible that says**: Luke 6:45 (Christian Standard Bible).

95 **As Dr. King put it**: King (1962–63). A quote pulled from King's sermon notes. King wrote many sermons on love, including this one, a draft from 1962–63 titled "Love in Action."

100 **I have shared a few fitness resources**: Many in-demand trainers now offer a variety of ways to access their daily workout routines. The full-body, high-intensity workouts provide a path toward holistic fitness. Their programs are also accessible because you can try the moves in these routines almost anywhere. If you have fifteen minutes and a yoga mat, you can get a daily workout that strengthens, tones, and protects your body. If you can get your hands on a pair of dumbbells, you'll unlock even more ways to get into superhuman shape. Two resources to get you started are All/Out Studio (https://www.alloutstudio.com/), for on-the-go workout video routines that can fit into any busy schedule; and Strava (https://www.strava.com/mobile), for anyone exploring ways to approach fitness with others; the latter app provides opportunities to follow friends and join Challenges.

101 ***Yoga Journal***: The website of *Yoga Journal* (https://www.yogajournal.com/) is a great place to start learning about yoga, a physical practice that elevates the mind and helps you connect your mind, body, and spirit. There is also great information on the specifics of breathing techniques that can be applied to the breathing superpower.

101 **an app like Calm**: Calm (https://www.calm.com/) is a sleep and sound meditation app that helps lower anxiety and stress while building a routine of focus and mental rejuvenation.

117 **One TED talk that has**: Carol Dweck's 2014 TED talk on the growth mindset, titled "The Power of Believing that You Can Improve," is available on the TED website at https://www.ted.com/talks/carol_dweck_the_power_of_believing_that_you_can_improve.

117 **One of my favorite quotes**: Dweck (2006), p. 25.

Chapter 8

140 **the danger of succumbing to fear**: Obama (2018), p. 43.

Chapter 9

147 **the podcast *Affirmation Pod***: This podcast, hosted by Josie Ong, is a simple way to examine your thoughts. Whether you just listen, or listen and journal, *Affirmation Pod* can open a number of mental pathways to reaffirming the best aspects of your life and your creative self. It is available at https://www.affirmationpod.com/.

148 **including one in 2017 from *Forbes***: Landrum (2017).

150 **One of my favorite reads on habits**: Clear (n.d.).

151 **author and entrepreneur Virginia Heffernan**: Heffernan (2019).

REFERENCES

Black, Brandon, and Shayne Hughes. 2017. *Ego Free Leadership: Ending the Unconscious Habits that Hijack Your Business*. Austin: Greenleaf Book Group.

Brown, Tim. 2009. *Change by Design: How Design Thinking Transforms and Inspires Innovation*. New York: HarperCollins.

Campbell, Joseph. 1968. *The Hero with a Thousand Faces*. 2nd ed. Princeton, NJ: Princeton University Press.

Campbell, Joseph, with Bill Moyers. 1991. *The Power of Myth*. New York: Anchor Books. First published 1988.

Clear, James. n.d. "5 Common Mistakes that Cause New Habits to Fail." Accessed September 17, 2020. https://jamesclear.com/habits-fail.

Clear, James. 2018. *Atomic Habits: An Easy and Proven Way to Build Good Habits and Break Bad Ones*. New York: Avery.

Crowe, Kelsey, and Emily McDowell. 2017. *There Is No Good Card for This: What to Say and Do When Life Is Scary, Awful, and Unfair to People You Love*. San Francisco: HarperOne.

Dweck, Carol S. 2006. *Mindset: The New Psychology of Success*. New York: Ballantine Books.

Fingeroth, Danny. 2004. *Superman on the Couch: What Superheroes Really Tell Us about Ourselves and Our Society*. New York: Continuum.

Glei, Jocelyn K., ed. 2013. *Manage Your Day-to-Day: Build Your Routine, Find Your Focus, and Sharpen Your Creative Mind*. Las Vegas: Amazon Publishing.

Goggins, David. 2018. *Can't Hurt Me: Master Your Mind and Defy the Odds*. N.p.: Lioncrest Publishing.

Heath, Dan, and Chip Heath. 2008. *Made to Stick: Why Some Ideas Survive and Others Die*. New York: Random House.

Heffernan, Virginia. 2019. "Tech Marketing Is Losing Its Cool." *Wired*, October 22, 2019. https://www.wired.com/story/tech-marketing-losing-its-cool/.

Kelley, Tom, with Jonathan Littman. 2001. *The Art of Innovation: Lessons in Creativity from IDEO, America's Leading Design Firm*. New York: Currency.

King, Martin Luther, Jr. 1962–63. Draft of chapter IV, “Love in Action.” The Martin Luther King, Jr., Research and Education Institute, Stanford University. https://kinginstitute.stanford.edu/king-papers/documents/draft-chapter-iv-love-action.

Landrum, Sarah. 2017. “Millennials Link Money with Happiness, but Not How You Expect.” *Forbes*, October 6, 2017. https://www.forbes.com/sites/sarahlandrum/2017/10/06/millennials-link-money-with-happiness-but-not-how-you-expect/#326e763ddd62.

Maxwell, John C. 2010. *Everyone Communicates, Few Connect: What the Most Effective People Do Differently*. Nashville: Thomas Nelson.

McKay, Brett, and Kate McKay. 2011. “How to Become Superhuman.” *The Art of Manliness*, January 2, 2011. Updated May 28, 2018. https://www.artofmanliness.com/articles/becoming-superhuman-in-2011/.

Mendelson, Scott. 2019. “‘Avengers: Endgame’ Tops ‘Avatar’ at Worldwide Box Office.” *Forbes*, July 20, 2019. https://www.forbes.com/sites/scottmendelson/2019/07/20/avengers-endgame-avatar-james-cameron-marvel-star-wars-force-awakens-titanic-jurassic-box-office/#767a7a73d12b.

Obama, Michelle. 2018. *Becoming*. New York: Crown.

Rosenberg, Robin S. 2013. “Our Fascination with Superheroes.” In *Our Superheroes, Ourselves*, edited by Rosenberg, 3–18. Oxford: Oxford University Press.

Rosenberg, Robin S., and Peter Coogan, eds. 2013. *What Is a Superhero?* Oxford: Oxford University Press.

Smith, Ned. 2019. “Who Says Creativity Can’t Be Learned?” Updated February 27, 2019. https://www.businessnewsdaily.com/2471-creativity-innovation-learned.html.

Sun Tzu. 2019. *The Art of War*. Translated by Michael Nylan. New York: Norton.

Vernon, Jamie L. 2017. “Understanding the Butterfly Effect.” *American Scientist* 105, no. 3 (May–June): 103. https://doi.org/10.1511/2017.105.3.130.

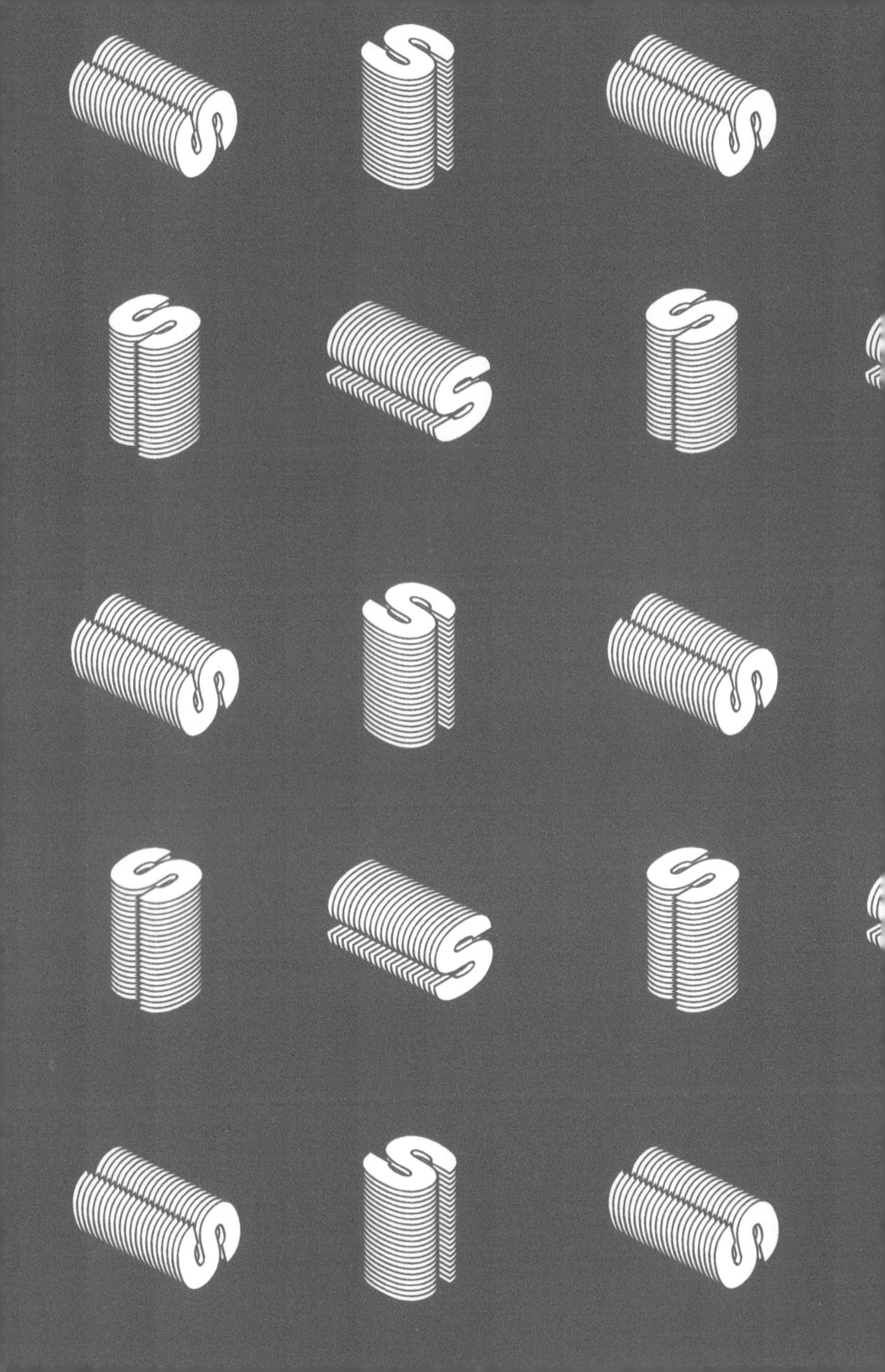

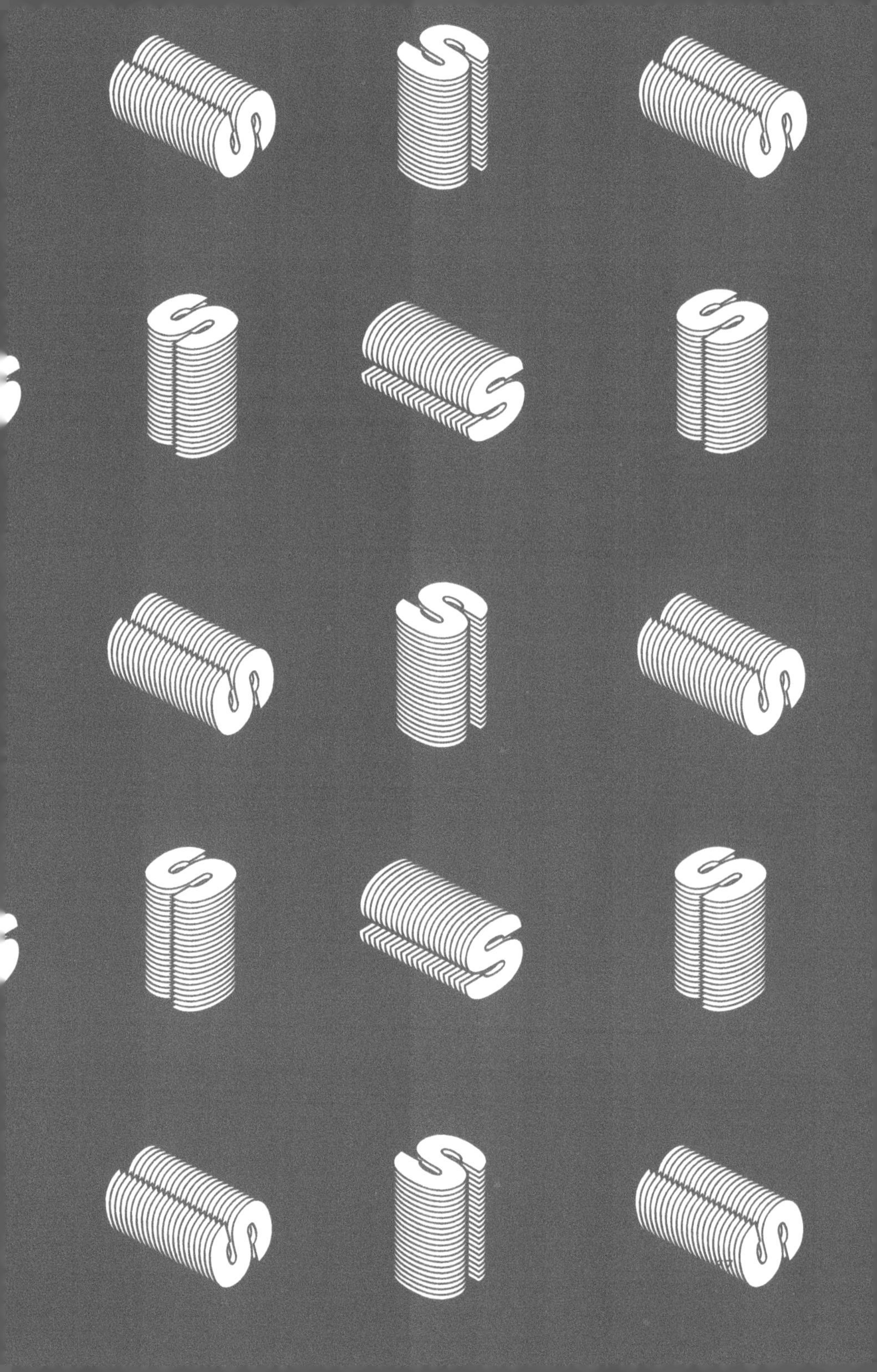

ABOUT THE AUTHOR

Donald Burlock serves as the Creative Technologist Lead of Physical Experience Design at Capital One. As a creative leader, he is committed to helping cross-functional, multidisciplinary teams evolve together to deliver game-changing customer experiences, whether app-based, hardware, or installations. He strongly believes that informed design strategy, elegant user experience, and ambitious content are the pillars by which brands can build equity, authenticity, and relatability.

During his more than ten years in creative strategy and product design, Donald has worked on many challenging and worthwhile projects, including the design, development, and global launch of the highly awarded Dolby Cinema program; content marketing and social media strategy for an augmented-reality motorcycle helmet; an onboarding app sequence for a med tech device; and brand content marketing programs for several global brands, including GE, Coca-Cola, Dolby, Cisco, and many startups in Silicon Valley. Prior to coming to the Bay Area in 2013, Donald spent time innovating with the design firm IDEO.

He holds a BS in Mechanical Engineering from Kettering University and a Master of Industrial Design degree from Georgia Institute of Technology.

CPSIA information can be obtained
at www.ICGtesting.com
Printed in the USA
LVHW010338111220
673819LV00039B/2578

9 781735 770208